LIVING BETWEEN
TWO
WORLDS

LIVING BETWEEN

TWO

WORLDS

JOEL S. GOLDSMITH

EDITED BY
LORRAINE SINKLER

1817

HARPER & ROW, PUBLISHERS
New York, Hagerstown, San Francisco, London

Library of Congress Cataloging in Publication Data

Goldsmith, Joel S., 1892–1964.
  Living between two worlds.

  1. Spiritual life. I. Title.
BL624.G64   1974   248'.4   73–18679
ISBN 0–06–063191–0

> Except the Lord build the house,
> they labour in vain that build it.
> —Psalm 127

Illumination dissolves all material ties and binds men together with the golden chains of spiritual understanding; it acknowledges only the leadership of the Christ; it has no ritual or rule but the divine, impersonal universal Love, no other worship than the inner Flame that is ever lit at the shrine of Spirit. This union is the free state of spiritual brotherhood. The only restraint is the discipline of Soul; therefore, we know liberty without license; we are a united universe without physical limits, a divine service to God without ceremony or creed. The illumined walk without fear—by Grace.

—The Infinite Way

Contents

CONTENTS

Itself Is Not Power—The Creative Intelligence Ordained Us for Its Purpose

Meditation Is the Way to Freedom—The Great Temptation: Accepting a Material Universe—Spiritual Discernment Reveals Infinity—Spiritual Discernment Reveals That Which Is

Spiritual Being Forms No Judgments—The Indestructible Relationship of Father and Son—The Death of Personal Sense Must Precede the Resurrection

Freedom Comes Through Conscious Oneness With Our Source—Consciousness Is the Source and Substance of Life—Material Sense Is a Sense of Separation From Consciousness

Right Identification—The Land of Milk and Honey or the Cross?—The Transition From This World to the Realm of Soul Is a Gradual One—Spiritual Fulfillment Is the Goal of the Way

Access to Omniscience and Divine Grace Through the Tran-

scendental Consciousness—Oneness, a Universal Truth—
Light-Bearers

To What Degree Will You Devote Yourself to Attaining
Christhood?—Choose Whether You Will Make God a Ser-
vant or Whether You Will Surrender to God's Will—Choose
Between Serving Good and Evil or Serving Omnipotence—
Choose To Accept Omnipresence As the Only Presence—
Choose To Claim No Qualities As Your Own—Choose To
Carry a Benediction Wherever You Go

The Universal Nature of Supply—Opening the Doors of Supply—Releasing Impersonal Love

Life More Abundant—Be a Benediction—Satisfy the Inner
Longing To Have Spiritual Identity Recognized—Bearing
Witness to the Christ-Identity—Conducting a Successful
Spiritual Healing Ministry—One World

Editor's Note

Living Between Two Worlds was a long time in being born. Early in 1964, along with other private papers, Joel Goldsmith sent me a page and a half, written in longhand, dated July 29, 1951, which reads as follows:

BETWEEN TWO WORLDS
by Joel S. Goldsmith

Dedicated to my students, some of whom have been with me since 1931 when I began revealing the secrets of the inner Kingdom.

You have understood so well what I have said from the inner Plane and have carried the Word as far as that understanding would permit you. Now the time has come to draw you closer to me and if possible draw you within that you might see this universe both from within and from without. In this way only will you really comprehend that which you have received in part and I have revealed in a measure. To fulfill your work in the world it is necessary to live on both planes—the inner and the outer—and to understand the life and law of Soul and body in order that you may teach those now looking to you for further guidance in spiritual development.

Thus far, I have guided, protected, and sustained your unfoldment —now you must undertake this Mission for your students. As you hear, feel, and read, you will find yourself drawn into the inner World where I am. Before this can be accomplished, there are preparations which must be made.

Then on March 30, 1964, Joel wrote me a letter which said in part:

You remember that about twelve years ago I sat in the airport in Seattle, and all of a sudden an unfoldment came and I wrote it down.

It was the beginning of a new book and I gave it the title "Between Two Worlds," but I never got much further than a page and one half of it, and every year it seems that I have looked at that page and one half and wondered what was next, but nothing would come. Then, yesterday morning, still on Maui, I awakened and I received a flood of unfoldment that gave me the whole rest of the book. I have no way of knowing just how this thing will unfold, but what I have done is this: The Easter Sunday tape has been given the title of "Between Two Worlds," and I will continue to use this title until I feel that I have reached the conclusion of it, and each Talk that I give that is to be typed will also be given the title "Between Two Worlds," so that when we are through we will have a series of tapes from which the book will evolve.

The unfoldment unlocked a door that heretofore has been completely locked. In fact, I think I wrote you last week from Maui that I really was facing a blank wall or another horizon, but actually it was more like a blank wall or a closed door, and the experience yesterday morning completely opened that door, dissolved the wall or the horizon, and I am sure that I can say that a whole new vision has been given me. Watch carefully the tapes that come forth beginning today, Easter Sunday.

The tapes to which Joel referred are the six reels of *The 1964 Oahu-Maui Series,** which became the 1967 *Letters* sent to students around the world. Now Joel's long-envisioned book, which he planned to dedicate to his students and which first came into form in the classes given on the islands of Oahu and Maui, is finally being published.

L.S.

*These tapes are available for purchase.

· 1 ·

Opening the Door to Infinity

CIVILIZATIONS HAVE COME AND GONE; civilizations have lived and died; and there is no guarantee that our present civilization will be permanent. At some future time, a new race of men may find parts of these cracker boxes we call buildings and homes, and they may even discover rock-and-roll records that bear witness to our state of civilization. The point is that just as other civilizations have passed from sight, so many more may also pass from sight before the truth that every mystic has revealed is discovered and demonstrated, which is that man has inherent within himself the capacity to surrender such protective measures as self-preservation and to open the door within his consciousness and receive the Spirit of God.

There are two levels of consciousness. There is the spiritual, incorporeal level as described in the first chapter of Genesis. On this level, man created in the image and likeness of God shows forth neither sin, disease, death, lack, limitation, nor any of man's

The material in this volume first appeared in the form of letters sent to students of The Infinite Way throughout the world, as an aid to living effectively in this world through a deeper understanding of Scripture and the principles of The Infinite Way.—ED.

inhumanity to man. Those born into the consciousness of the first chapter of Genesis have neither father nor mother. They are the Melchizedek-consciousness: they are not physical offspring, and they have no human parentage. They are incorporeal.

But those born of human parents are born into the level of the second-chapter-of-Genesis creation, the world of mind, the mortal consciousness of good and evil, which constitutes humanhood. It is this humanhood that makes us think that by destroying our enemy or competitor we can live and prosper, or that by taking away somebody's freedom we can become greater.

A leaven is necessary to break through the crust of self-preservation. This leaven is the Spirit of God in man, which, when It* is raised up, lifts man to Its level; and then, instead of "man, whose breath is in his nostrils,"[1] we now have the son of God, that man who has his being in Christ.

The Master acknowledged that there are two men: the man of earth—the creature, the mortal, the viper—and the divine Presence within individual consciousness which, when recognized and released, changes man from the man of earth to the son of God. He revealed that it is necessary for man to be ordained and lifted up by the Spirit. Man cannot be spiritualized by means of a diploma or a license; he cannot be ordained by an organization. External forms of worship do not contribute to a person's spiritual life and development except in proportion as the outer rite is accompanied by an inner Spirit or Grace. It is the experience of the Presence Itself that is necessary for spiritual progress. While

*In the spiritual literature of the world, the varying concepts of God are indicated by the use of such words as "Father," "Mother," "Soul," "Spirit," "Principle," "Love," and "Life." Therefore, in this book the author has used the pronouns "He" and "It," or "Himself" and "Itself," interchangeably in referring to God.

we cannot see, hear, taste, touch, or smell the Spirit of God, we can experience It by opening the inner door.

OPENING THE DOOR
LEADS TO GREATER ACTIVITY AND INNER PEACE

Meditation is the key that opens the door. "I stand at the door, and knock."[2] This *I** is God, and the door is within us, but it is not a door to the external world. It is a door leading within to deeper realms of our self. By opening the door, we become aware of a realm, an activity, a law, which in spiritual language has been called "meat," "bread," "wine," "water," the substance of all life and of all form. We open the door within our consciousness so that there may be released from within us the Invisible, the Spirit of God in man.

Once we have reached or touched the inner kingdom, we are no longer living unto ourselves, not even living unto our families exclusively, but we are participating more actively in the affairs of the world, and in those things that make for a happier, more successful, and more peaceful way of life. The kingdom of God does not deal with something separate and apart from living. The kingdom of God concerns itself with our daily life. It is not meant to take us out of the world, but rather to leave us in the world, separate and apart from its negative aspects.

The very *I* that is standing knocking at the door of our consciousness brings us "peace . . . not as the world giveth,"[3] but *My*** peace, the peace of *I*. There is no use looking outside and wondering in what form that peace will come, because it does not

*The word "I," italicized, refers to God.
**The word "My," capitalized, refers to God.

3

come in a worldly form. Strangely enough, however, when the inner peace comes it forms and re-forms our outer life. It changes our relationships with other human beings. It changes the nature and the amount of our supply because it is Its function to see that we are fed and clothed abundantly. All things will be added unto us but they will not be added by taking thought for the things:

Relinquish thought of things; turn within and admit Me. * *Open the inner door of your consciousness that* I *may enter the temple of your being, for in reality* I *am the temple of your being;* I *am the Lord of your being. Relax and rest and be a beholder as* I, *the Spirit of God in you, go before you to prepare the way. This is* My *function. For this purpose have* I *planted the seed of my Self within you. For this purpose have* I *breathed* My *life into you.* **

In our work, the emphasis is not on trying to be more loving, more just, or more gracious. Our entire attention is centered on admitting the Spirit, and then It will be more loving and gracious through us. It will be expressing patience and benevolence within us. We will not have to take thought for things: we will be instruments for Its grace and glory. We will bear witness not to our own goodness or our own benevolences: we will bear witness to God's grace functioning in us.

*The word "Me," capitalized, refers to God.

**The italicized portions are spontaneous meditations that came to the author during periods of uplifted consciousness and are not in any sense intended to be used as affirmations, denials, or formulas. They have been inserted in this book from time to time to serve as examples of the free flowing of the Spirit. As the reader practices the Presence, he, too, in his exalted moments, will receive ever new and fresh inspiration as the outpouring of the Spirit.

EXPERIENCE IS THE PROOF OF TRUTH

The entire foundation of The Infinite Way rests on attaining the actual experience of the Presence. Quotations from the Bible and other sources are used in my writings to illustrate principles, but they are not offered as proof. The revelations and unfoldments which have been given to me are being passed on to you and shared with you merely as my experience. Any proof as to their rightness has to come through your own experience because—and on this point I am sure that Scripture will never be changed— "neither will they be persuaded, though one rose from the dead." [4] You must not expect that your relatives or friends will believe. They will find some coincidence that will explain the fruitage that is yours. If you experience the presence of God, it will be proof to you, however, and, what is more, it will give you the principle whereby you can help your neighbor, friend, and family, even without their acknowledgment or recognition.

There is a Spirit in man. This Spirit ordains, heals, resurrects, lifts up, and illumines, but It must be experienced. The way is through practicing the presence of God and through meditation. The more we live in the remembrance of the words of mystical literature and Scripture, the more we live in the awareness of the Spirit and Its function, the nearer we bring ourselves to the actual experience.

Practicing the Presence brings about an inner quiet and stillness, at least in a greater measure than we have heretofore known. It brings the day nearer when the experience comes, and we understand what the Master meant when he said, "The Spirit of the Lord is upon me, because he hath anointed me." [5]

SYMBOLS OF THE HIGHER CONSCIOUSNESS

The higher consciousness is shown forth in many ways. Throughout mystical literature, we read of robes, and we have been told that the Master wore a white seamless robe, meaning that his consciousness was robed in the seamless wholeness and incorporeal purity of Spirit.

The Robe has always had a mystical meaning. There are white robes that describe the ultimate, incorporeal Spirit of God in man. There is the purple robe of royalty which is a state of consciousness indicating more of temporal power than of spiritual. There are the yellow robes, commonly used by holy men in the Orient. All these serve to indicate states of consciousness. We are not concerned with whether we are adorned with material robes, however, but we are concerned that we be always robed in the Spirit.

There is the jeweled ring symbolizing the authority of the son of God, the ring that is sometimes kissed as an acknowledgment of divine authority. No ring itself has power, but kissing a ring outwardly or kissing it inwardly invisibly could have power if it were done in the recognition of that jewel which is without "price," [6] the Word which is without form. Any acknowledgment of that indwelling Word is equivalent to the outer ceremony of the kissing of the ring.

Outer communion is the experience of opening the inner door, where "I and my Father" [7] can commune, not as if we were two beings, but as the Father revealing Itself as the deeper nature of the Self of our own being. It is a communion which takes place when the Spirit of the Lord God is upon us, and we are consciously aware of a spiritual Presence.

When we become aware of that Spirit of the Lord God being

6

upon us, it is as if we had been washed clean, as if a baptism had taken place. It is like a strong, yet gentle, flow of water touching us in the without, but at the same time as if this stream of water were permeating us within, flowing through the veins. This is indeed a baptism of the Spirit. Its outer symbol is pure water, but that baptism has no value except as it may be accompanied by the inner experience.

The oneness of "I and my Father" is an inner experience in which the Spirit of God blends with our spirit, the life of God becomes our life, and even our body becomes the temple of God. This is the spiritual oneness that takes place as a result of the opening of consciousness.

Consciousness can be opened in two ways. One, very rare, and experienced by only a few persons in the history of the world, is when God opens the door of our consciousness without any help from us. The other is where the door is opened through meditation, communion, and through an inner ability to dwell with the Spirit. There is an experience that takes place within that testifies to the fact that we are one with the Father and all that the Father has is ours.

Repeating words or thinking thoughts is a waste of time, except as it may lead to the actual experience. Faith in the power of some arrangement of words is as futile as faith in a golden calf. Whether we externalize a golden calf or whether we have a golden calf internally in the form of statements or words or thoughts, we are equally far afield.

Thoughts are legitimate, words are legitimate, knowing the letter of truth is legitimate, but only as steppingstones to the experience of the inner Presence. When, in our meditation, we have opened the door of consciousness and have felt the Presence enter—and we do not look for It in form, because this would be just another golden calf, but we expect It in the form of an awareness, an assurance, a peace—we can be sure that God is on the field.

Spiritual healing takes place only when the Spirit of God bears witness within the consciousness of whoever may be praying. Prayer or treatment separate and apart from the experience of the presence of God does not heal. On the other hand, the experience of the presence of God very often makes prayer or treatment unnecessary. Infinite Way practitioners are taught to have no reliance whatsoever on prayer or treatment unless they feel that the Spirit of God is bearing witness with them and they receive an inner release.

Sometimes the Voice Itself may declare, "This is my beloved child, all is well"; or, "*I* am on the field. *I* will never leave you or forsake you." But whether it comes in a tangible way such as a voice or in some other form, there must be an inner assurance that God is on the scene. Otherwise, the prayer or the treatment is of no avail. This is equally true in the spiritual work we do in connection with our family, business, artistic, or professional life. The actual experience of the Presence must be felt within us. When it is, the miracle takes place in the outer realm.

A Complete Surrender of All Human Traits and Human Solutions Is Necessary

Another reason for lack of healing is that very often we are seeking healing instead of wholeness. To seek healing means to desire to be rid of some ill, some pain, some discord, some malformation, or some inharmony. This is no way to go to God. The only right way to go to God is for the experience of completeness in God, and this means the willingness that we be washed clean of the human traits to which each one of us clings. We all have human traits we would gladly be rid of, but there may be others that we will permit no man to take from us, and those are the very ones that are the barriers to healing.

As we observe to what extent we would like to substitute a good human condition for an evil one, we will know why our prayers are not answered. To go to a spiritual God to find a human solution based on human ideas of what is right is futile. We must be willing to surrender all concepts as to the solution of any problem because success comes only with the surrender of material or human desires and the desire for God's government on earth. But when we open our consciousness to a spiritual solution, it comes forth in a human way that we could never have thought of or planned. Going to God for wholeness—the wholeness of the Robe, the completeness of the Spirit, the actual Baptism—means a willingness to be thoroughly washed inside and out.

Spiritual healing is a beautiful activity if we can rise above the desire to heal someone, if we can rise above pity for a person's diseases and pains, or if we can rise above trying to lift someone out of his distress. Even if we succeeded, ninety-nine out of one hundred persons would go back into something worse. But where there is a transformation of consciousness, that is something else.

The metaphysical state of consciousness in which, for the most part, there is a concern with effects—demonstrating health, supply, purity, or the overcoming of false appetites—is no part of mysticism. In mysticism, we seek only the attainment of that "mind . . . which was also in Christ Jesus," [8] the attainment of the Robe, the whole man.

Until there is a recognition that there is an *I* standing at the door of consciousness, there is no possibility of entering the mystical kingdom. When there is that recognition, however, consciousness is immediately opened to receive the Spirit, and eventually we come to that place where we can say with Paul: " 'I live; yet not I, but Christ liveth in me.' [9] That indwelling Presence is living my life."

Opening consciousness to the inflow of the *I* gives us a keener ability in the market place or in the arts and professions, because this fourth-dimensional consciousness not only activates us but motivates us to thinking in terms of the universal good rather than the personal. We have moved in consciousness from the man of earth to spiritual man.

The new discoveries of Scripture corroborate the correctness of the idea of the "two men," the man of earth and the spiritual man, and the nature of that which brings to light in the man of earth the spiritual man. The metaphysical world has not accepted the idea of two men. Instead, it has insisted that a human being is spiritual and perfect, which is ludicrous when we witness the person it is calling spiritual and perfect.

In the Bible, man is identified in his twofold nature, the man of earth who must put off mortality and put on immortality "that mortality might be swallowed up of life." [10] This, we are told, is attained by a transformation of consciousness. That transformation can be brought about through either direct intervention of God as in the case of Moses on the mountaintop or through the intercession of a spiritual teacher. When Jesus said, "Call no man your father upon the earth," [11] he was revealing that the creative Principle of one is the same for all. Therefore we all must be equal, but not in forms of expression. Beauty is found not only in a rose. We can see beauty in a stone or in a piece of wood. So, also, we have to see that intelligence is God-bestowed, but we will not all express the same amount of it. Intelligence is stored up within us, but the amount we express is determined by how much we draw forth.

THE POWER OF SILENCE

By our living of the principles of truth, without speaking of them, others witness what takes place and are led to us. This is the principle of the Infinite Invisible. We do not have to speak truth; we do not have to advertise it. We have to live it, and then it spreads out from us without our being aware of how it happened. None of us knows why people are influenced in the direction of truth. The only thing we do know is that it is not humanly induced.

The greatest power on earth is the power of silence. Spiritual power cannot be expressed in words or thoughts, nor can it come through words or thoughts. Only through silence, when the senses are at rest, can spiritual power be released. That is why, whether we are in prayer for some problem of our own or for that of another, or whether it is on the wider level of the nation or the world, the rehearsing in our mind of basic spiritual principles is only a step leading to a period of absolute silence in which that invisible Spirit can come through.

If we are not careful, we will be trapped in the belief in temporal power, the power of numbers or the power of some human "do-good" activity. In the period that lies just ahead, let us remember to open ourselves to a spiritual grace instead of trying to work out the "rights and wrongs" of any problem, personal or national. In this way, we may be able to introduce Something that will change the picture.

Some day it will have to be proved that "ten" righteous men

can save a city.[12] When? I do not know, but it could be today. Spiritually, it is still true that we must "put up again [our] sword into his place." Spiritually it is still true that "they that take the sword shall perish with the sword." [13] Therefore, if Steinmetz's prophecy that in this century spiritual power will be proved is to come true, now is the time to prove it. Spiritual power means introducing the Spirit of God into the situation—not to prove right or wrong—and then letting the chips fall where they may.

Let us not have any "golden calf" in our mind, any images or reliances. Let us have a receptive consciousness and then what comes is with signs following. If we receive an answer that is a blessing universally, it is from God because neither the devil nor personal sense can be responsible for purely good action universally.

When we enter meditation and close our eyes to "this world," [14] let us remember that we are now in the corridor, or at least we are behind the door that opens to Infinity. Through our consciousness, we have access to the infinity of God, the activity of God, the substance and the law of God. All this is within us.

Let us enter into meditation and go to the Spirit for the purpose of enlightenment, with a complete freedom from concepts, and then receive the truth that in the presence of God there is fulfillment and freedom, freedom from any sense of limitation.

· 2 ·

The Nature of Spiritual Attainment

IN MAN'S EARLY EXPERIENCE ON THIS EARTH, all his activities were on the physical level of life: farming, road building, fighting, fishing, and hunting; and he was living purely on the physical and emotional level. Gradually, however, the world groped toward an understanding of the mind and eventually discovered its potentialities, and along with the discovery and development of the mental realm, access to the cosmic realm was also found. That is why during the less than one hundred years just past such great strides have been made in invention, science, discovery, and knowledge. These discoveries in science and the new forms of art, literature, and music have come forth from the cosmic storehouse, and, as access is gained to that storehouse, the universal mind gives up its wisdom and reveals what men are seeking, whether a way to the North or South Pole, a way to fly in the air or to travel under water, or whether they are seeking new machinery for further automation.

The entire nature of human living has been changed because we are no longer confined to what our ancestors knew. Now we have access to Infinity, and there is no limit to what can be achieved through our understanding of the truth that we can

13

reach the universal storehouse of the laws of life: physical or material laws, mental laws, laws of nature, all those laws governing automobiles and airplanes, and laws governing new ways of raising crops. So we come to the age in which we will be able to live without limitation.

When man recognizes that he has access to the entire cosmic realm, he will bring to light a whole new world, glimpses of which we have already seen in what has been accomplished in the last fifty years and which is only the beginning of a still greater era.

THE FRUITAGE OF THE MIND, AN UNCERTAIN QUANTITY

But while the world was progressing from the physical realm of life to the mental, the religious life of man remained in *status quo*. True, during this time there were mystics who revealed spiritual truth, but all too seldom did this find its way to the public. So, until the religious mental sciences were brought forth, which were the mental aspect of man expanding and finding new principles, the majority of people have continued to live the religious life of four thousand or two thousand years ago with very few signs of any change. But just as inventors and scientists have found a whole new world through the mind, so metaphysicians have discovered the new world of the mind applicable to phases of human existence other than invention and science.

All this indicates progress. Then one day we awaken to the truth that the realm of the mind we have discovered can be used for both good and evil. All these discoveries have their good aspects and their evil ones. Electricity that gives us heat, cold, and comfort also kills or can be used to kill. The discovery of atomic secrets which eventually will free the world from most of its physical labors can be used to destroy life. Dynamite, which originally was used as a means of helping to carve out cities from the country, to clear the land for the planting of crops, and in other useful ways, can also be used for destructive purposes.

Access to the cosmic universal mind of man is a wondrous thing in one sense, but frightening in another, because whether or not these great discoveries are ultimately used for the welfare of mankind depends on the moral nature of man. And the moral nature of man with a few exceptions here and there has never been above that of self-interest, self-preservation, or self-profit.

Only when a spiritual element enters the consciousness of an individual does he lose the capacity to bring forth new forms for evil purposes, but until man finds a way to bring the spiritual element into the consciousness of mankind, he is at the mercy of those who govern, control, or lead. We have already seen that in this era of unbelievable scientific discoveries these great accomplishments have not lessened our fears or dangers, but rather have they increased them.

No one today can truthfully say he is happier or safer or more free because of these great scientific advances. More comfortable, yes, of course. Most of us in the Western world are living with tiled bathrooms, electricity, air conditioning, and all the other comforts of life, but is mankind happier, safer, or freer? In the free countries of the world, the private life of the citizens has come increasingly under government surveillance. Man is more controlled by his government today than he was fifty years ago, and he can never forget that if it is not his own government that is a threat to his personal liberty, there is always one just across the ocean or the border. Inventions, discoveries, and great material progress have not given our world greater individual freedom, peace, or safety. There is no need to point out that in spite of all the great advances that have been made, there is now a need to build more mental institutions than ever before.

Life has not become easier for people. For some of them it has become more comfortable physically, but the burdens many persons carry in the mind are greater, and they come largely from fear of the very discoveries that should have set them free.

TOTAL MORALITY ALONE CAN SAFEGUARD
THE USE OF MENTAL DISCOVERIES

As long as we remain in the mental or cosmic realm of the universal mind, we remain in the realm of good and evil. Why learn the secrets of mind and then find that sometimes they are used for the purpose of malpractice? Why learn the laws of mind and then discover that they are used for propaganda or advertising purposes and not necessarily advertising of the right nature?

Today, we do have access to the mind; we have access to the laws that govern nature. The next step we must take is to gain access to the world of morals. I am not speaking merely of sexual morality, but of morality in its wider sense, of the morality that should govern business, art, literature, government, and all our human relationships. We must find access to total morality in order that these great discoveries may eventually be used by man solely for a productive and fulfilled life.

It is only when an Element that is not human, that is neither physical nor mental, enters consciousness that our moral or spiritual capacity is developed. It is Something that renders it impossible for anyone to do evil to another consciously, or to work for the injury or the loss of others. The introduction of this Element into consciousness marks the beginning of a new era.

All human beings live by the law of self-preservation, which is considered the natural law of mankind. That is what makes it

16

possible to legalize war and, according to this age-old law, makes it perfectly moral to destroy someone else to protect ourselves. That has become ingrained as a human way of life. The idea, too, of influencing the public by any means, regardless of the nature of the harm it may do, seems to be an underlying principle of much advertising. "Let the buyer beware" is still the guideline for many businesses. This cannot change until that new Element enters human consciousness. First, however, we must discover a way to bring that Element into our own consciousness, because until we become aware of the fact that there is a transcendental power and a way of introducing it into our consciousness, we cannot live by it and we cannot teach it to others.

Is there a God-power that can be brought into human existence to change the nature of man so that in the mind of man there will be no desire to use these powers—whether they be the power of the atom, of hypnotism, or of propaganda—to enslave the world? That is the question. Most people on earth have not even reached the stage of real conviction that there is God. They might say that they believe in God, but an absolute conviction that there is God? Very few on earth have this.

There is God. But how do we bring this God into our individual experience and thereby discover that if we can bring It into our experience we have the assurance that eventually It will function in the experience of all mankind? If I cannot prove God in a measure for myself, I have no way of proving It for you. If I cannot in a tiny measure demonstrate the presence and power of God in my individual experience, I cannot share the experience with you because I have nothing to share; I am barren.

So with you. You have a household; you have a family; you have friends. It would be ludicrous for you to talk to them about the God you believe in, the God you are convinced of, until you have discovered the way to bring the activity of God into your individual experience. Then you would not have to tell them about it. They would see it. That is why, when you really experience God, you do not have to advertise or proselyte: you merely have to be, and you will soon discover that those who are seeking that level of life will find you. Otherwise you will have many heartaches by giving your "pearls" to the unprepared thought and having them thrown back at you.

As we go back to the revelations of the mystics, we discover not only that God is, but that the spiritual might of God is within you and within me. To understand that is to come to a place where we can set about opening our consciousness to the experience of the Presence.

THE DIVINE CONSCIOUSNESS REVEALS ITSELF AS THE TEACHER IN A MOMENT OF READINESS

The Master revealed that the physical act of baptism is but a symbol of the real baptism, and so every time that any individual receives baptism—the visitation or the ordination of the Spirit— that individual immediately is an instrument through which It is imparted to others who seek It. That seeking must be real. It must not be for some personal motive or purpose: it must be for the experience of the grace of God. Then when we open our consciousness to receive that Grace, we make ourselves receptive to It, and somewhere in the world there is a spiritualized consciousness to impart It to us.

There is an old saying that when the student is ready the teacher will appear. Too many believe that this means when the student is ready some human teacher is going to come along to instruct

18

him. It really does not mean that at all. There are far too few real spiritual teachers in the world, and these few humanly could not possibly reach all those who are seeking.

The statement means that when we in our hearts and souls desire to know God aright, to receive God's grace, to be freed of our sins, false appetites, hates, enmities, jealousies, and other human traits, when we are really ready to be made spiritually whole, the teacher will appear. It may be a teacher ten thousand miles away sitting in meditation who knows nothing about us personally and of whom we know nothing personally, and yet we receive our grace and our freedom. There is nothing personal in the spiritual kingdom, so we may never know the teacher who reached us, and the teacher may never know us or know that we were reached by his meditation. It is entirely the activity of God-consciousness.

Whether or not there is a human teacher available is of no importance because when we are ready for God-consciousness, our teacher, the divine Consciousness, will appear and set us free. If a spiritual teacher were limited to helping those who come within range of his physical presence, there would be very few helped on earth, and strangely enough, many of those who do have the good fortune to come into the presence of a spiritual teacher may not be ready to receive their freedom or enlightenment, and, therefore, do not receive it.

GRATITUDE, THE TANGIBLE SIGN OF READINESS

The effort students put into acquiring truth determines what they will get out of it. In The Infinite Way, I have observed many persons who listen to lectures, read books, go to classes, and accomplish nothing. Why? Because they put nothing into it. The whole secret of life is in outpouring. When a person has been touched by the Spirit, we do not have to teach or even tell him this.

There are signs that indicate the measure of a student's readiness and, although most of these signs are not tangible, they are something a teacher feels. One sign of spiritual endowment, however, is always present: there is gratitude; there is love; there is sharing. A teacher can always tell when a student is beginning to be inspired by the Spirit because the student's nature changes in that regard. Where formerly he may have "paid a bill," now he shows signs of a tenderness where gratitude is concerned. He could then no more be ungrateful than he could be immoral.

A teacher cannot tell students to be grateful. All he can do is to bring out what the principle is and show them the basis from which he is working. A teacher cannot teach anyone to be moral. He does not tell students they must stop smoking, stop drinking, or stop anything else. This is none of his business. His business is to impart the Spirit and let It do the purifying.

Infinite Way teachers are not trying to improve anyone's humanhood. They are not concerning themselves with whether a student is moral or whether he is grateful. What they are concerned with is this: Is the student seeking spiritual light? Then they can proceed to the major theme of The Infinite Way, the impartation of the Spirit.

Final freedom will not come until the spiritual Influence has entered the consciousness of man so that he will not only be empowered with spiritual grace to do good, but will at the same time lose the capacity to think evil, much less do it.

THE REQUIREMENT FOR ILLUMINATION

Is it not clear that the demonstration of spiritual harmony is an individual matter and that the only demonstration to be made is a change of consciousness? Therefore, attaining health or supply is an individual demonstration of consciousness, and even if a hundred of us attained it, the one hundred first might not. Our goal is that the material state of consciousness "die" and that the spiritual state of consciousness be born. If we can succeed with that, all the rest will be added. If we cannot succeed in the transformation of consciousness, the things will not be added.

The Infinite Way stands alone in that it cannot promise anything to anyone. But if a person is seeking a change of consciousness, with that, we can help him. What it does for him, we have no way of knowing. Each of us has to be purged of whatever illusions he may have. Some of us look on health and certain means of income as natural, and we have to lose that reliance and attitude. In other words, we are in the process of losing our material sense of things and being reborn into the spiritual sense of things.

There is a requisite for illumination, and that is the desire to be made whole: not merely physically healthy, financially abundant, or happy in relationships. The Infinite Way is based entirely on attaining spiritual consciousness, letting it unfold, and the life lived be the testimony of the measure of its attainment.

Nothing can be accomplished without the attainment of spiritual consciousness, so the question is: "How do I attain it? How do I attain it more quickly?" The Master cautioned, "Strait is the gate, and narrow is the way, which leadeth unto life, and few there be that find it." [1] Jesus knew that the way is not easily attained, because the moment we think of attaining spiritual light, some way by which we hope to benefit from it enters our mind. Some want it for health, for supply, or for companionship, and some want it for peace on earth.

This brings us to self-surrender, which means surrendering those things we think we want, whatever it is we are looking for in life. Let us surrender all desire because that is the barrier to the major attainment. If we go to God wanting health, wealth, or something else, we are going to God as a beggar, and we are unwittingly accusing Him of withholding.

The gifts of God are not material. There is no way for a human being to know the nature of God's gifts because the only way a human being has of knowing is to look around and judge by what others have, and that is not the nature of the kingdom of God.

"My kingdom is not of this world." [2] What would happen if we could eradicate from our thought the kingdom of man and go into meditation in the same way the early explorers went to the North and South Poles, not knowing what they would find, only knowing: "I do not know what to pray for, because I do not know what the kingdom of God is like, and I do not know what God has to give"?

Very often it shocks me when I am called upon for help in serious cases and think of all the people dying from accidents, cancer, or polio, and I remember that God is doing nothing about it, that God does not care "two hoots." Yes, it shocks me, but out of that shock comes the ability to say: "I do not know what I am going to You for, but here I am."

How useless it would be to go to God to save someone's life when others are dying! How horrible it would be to go to God for supply for someone when hundreds of people are starving! If we can eliminate from our thought the idea of saving people's lives,

22

bringing them supply, or getting them out of prison, and can realize: "Thy grace is my sufficiency, and I do not know what Thy grace is," miracles will take place in our experience.

It helps me to know that God is Spirit because that frees me from all attempts to draw forth anything of a material nature from God. God is Spirit, and I have to rest on that. Whatever God's grace is, whatever God's gift is, it must be spiritual. It appears to us in some material form, because we still have material concepts of the spiritual kingdom, but it is never material. When we experience a physical healing, in our ignorance we say, "My body has been made well." We think a sick body has been made well. No, the body of God has been revealed.

If we could only see supply as it really is, we would know it is not money. As a matter of fact, the kingdom of God is incorporeal, and therefore, God's gift is incorporeal. When we say, "This is more or better matter," we have not recognized, "This is still spiritual, in spite of appearances."

Awakening to the Spiritual Impulse

Each one of us who has come this far on the Path has an obligation to the world. That obligation is to open our consciousness continuously until we receive the Spirit of God, until It is let loose within us, until It takes over our life and frees us from the sense of self-preservation and lifts us, if possible, into the way revealed by Christ Jesus of laying down our life that someone else may live. It is not taking someone else's life that we may live or taking someone else's property that we may prosper. We lay down our life that others may live. Neither you nor I in our human state of consciousness have the capacity to be so noble, so let us not live in a world of imagination and believe that that is what we would do, because of ourselves we would not and could not. If the time comes when we would or when we do, be assured that by that time we have received the ordination of the Spirit, and we are no longer doing it of ourselves but it is that we can do all things through Christ, even to the sacrifice of personal selfhood.

There is a Spirit in man, and this Spirit is just as much in the most evil man as in the most humanly good man. But this Spirit must be awakened. "Awake thou that sleepest, and arise from the dead, and Christ shall give thee light."[3] Awake! "Rise, take up thy bed, and walk." [4] This spiritual influence is a dormant influence that must be awakened, and despite all the help we may receive, the major responsibility rests with us to bring ourselves to the point of conviction that we wish to be made spiritually whole, that we wish to live our life by the grace of God and not by personal sense. In proportion as we reach that point, our teacher appears. The divine Consciousness, which is manifest in some individual somewhere on this side of the veil or the other, reaches us, and we are set free.

· 3 ·

Easter, a Rising Out
of Material Sense

THE MAJOR PRINCIPLE OR REVELATION OF THE INFINITE WAY is
that God is consciousness, and that infinite divine Consciousness
forms Itself as individual being, as my individual consciousness
and yours, not a portion of It, but all of It.

Most persons have been taught that man begins from a seed,
and they have been led to believe that there is something not quite
spiritual about the whole idea of conception and birth. They have
thought of creation as an act of man and woman, about which
there has always lurked some feeling of wrongness, and in *their*
sense of creation there is something wrong because it means that
they are accepting man as a creator. But man is not a creator, and
the belief that he is has given rise to the idea that man is brought
forth in sin and in iniquity.

The truth is that the activity of creation begins with the Spirit
of God pouring into individual consciousness as love. That divine
love pours from your consciousness into your mind and tangibly
it brings unto you your own with whom you are one, and then the
idea of love, union, and oneness comes forth as the creation of the
next generation. There is nothing sinful, nothing evil, nothing

25

finite, nothing mortal about it at all. It all has its beginning in conscious union with God.

While there cannot be a material creation because God is the only creator and God is Spirit, a material sense of creation has been entertained, and that is where this whole feeling of sin or wrongness comes from. All human experience has its foundation in a *material sense* of a spiritual universe. What is called the immorality and delinquency of this age has its basis in that same material sense, because since our young people have not been taught to understand that their first duty every day is to establish their conscious oneness with the Source so that they are animated throughout the day and the night by the Spirit, they have sought satisfaction on the level of mind and body. Thus they are led into all kinds of pleasures and pastimes which eventuate in what the world calls sin. None of this could happen if an individual realized on waking in the morning:

God is Spirit, and that Spirit is the animating consciousness of my being. It is the Spirit of God that permeates my soul, mind, and body, and supplies me with Its creations.

With such a realization each morning, the whole mind and body would be devoted during the day to letting spiritual unfoldment take place, and both mind and body would be led in the right direction.

Material Sense Results in Limitation

A material sense of spiritual creation has led to a material sense of supply, and because of that, prayers are uttered to God asking for food, clothing, housing, and supply, whereas the principle is that the earth is full of God's glory, whether it appears as vegetables, fruits, fish, birds, or whatnot.

If, instead of thinking that this abundance has to be divided, we realized, "Son, thou art ever with me, and all that I have is thine," [1] then, rather than looking at the possessions of others and desiring them, we would be living in the awareness that through our consciousness we have access to Infinity. This Infinity will pour into our consciousness spiritually, take form in our mind mentally, and then appear externally in what is called material form.

A human being is living in a purely *material sense* of world, but he is not living in a material world because there is none. All that exists is Spirit and Spirit's creation, about which the human race entertains a materialistic concept. This is the experience of the Prodigal who wandered away from the Father's house where everything was his by divine right. He wandered out into a world of limitation where he believed he could create an empire of his own.

For a time such empires flourish—national empires and family empires—but none of them has ever been permanent. If any of them had been permanent, by now the descendants of powerful and ruthless rulers of the past would probably own all the world. In modern times, the families of some of our financial and industrial giants who have built commercial empires would eventually own and control whole nations. But all accumulations of material resources and power always break because there is something inherent in the situation which brings that about. Emerson explained it in this way, "The dice of God are always loaded," * and when the overbearing get too

*See Chapter Seven in the author's *The Contemplative Life* (New York: Julian Press, 1963).

27

overbearing, the empire cracks beneath them.

What we must realize is that God is appearing as spiritual man, but that we are now entertaining a materialistic concept of God and man. Let us begin with creation and birth so that we can see that man does not evolve from a seed. Man, that is, individual being, has his beginning in God-consciousness expressing Itself as love, joy, beauty, and truth. All these enter the mind as what we call love, drawing man to woman, and in that union enabling the spiritual activity of God to form Itself through the mind as love and through the body as a seed, even though we must acknowledge that there was a time when there was no seed, and therefore, when there was only the consciousness of God.

Through the medium of individual consciousness, expressing as the mind and body, the next generation is brought forth in the image and likeness of God with the characteristics and the nature of God. The child inherits even the name of God and eventually knows itself as I and calls itself I, which is the name of the Father.

As children learn that God is really their Father and that God has given unto them his name of *I*, so that all that *I*, the Father, has, I, the son, has, they grow up without a materialistic sense. They develop and mature, showing forth the glory that they had in the beginning with God, knowing only God as their Father, teacher, supporter, supplier, knowing only the infinite nature of spiritual good and learning to let this take form. Then there will not be persons born to be artists doing bookkeeping for a living or bookkeepers trying to be artists, or persons born to be creative geniuses working in a factory. Because of conscious union with God, each person's destiny will unfold, and each will be fulfilled as was intended in the beginning in the mind of God.

Once you understand that God is the author of all creation, you

28

will know that God has a part for every character in His book and for every actor in His play. God has given to each his own destiny. But unless a person is taught to turn within each day for direction and guidance, he will not know what his destiny is, and he will be living in a materialistic sense of life where he has to provide for himself.

It is the materialistic sense of life that has brought forth the law of heredity. The only law of heredity there really is, however, is the law of divine inheritance. We are heirs of God, joint-heirs to all the heavenly riches.

Materialistically there is quantity and there is quality, but spiritually there is allness; spiritually there is oneness. Spiritually there is God, or Consciousness, and that cannot be divided or separated from Itself. Allness is given to the son, not a measure of it. If you look at life materialistically, you cannot understand this because from that point of view you see only division and separation. That the Infinite can be infinite and at the same time individual is incomprehensible to most persons.

Close your eyes and realize that you are not alone inside your own being. In the silence that reigns within, you have access to Infinity. *I*, Infinity, stand at the door of your consciousness and knock. You must open the door of your consciousness and bid It enter. Then you have access to Allness and are in direct union with It. The mind of God is now your mind. The whole being of God is pouring Itself into and through your individual consciousness. But since there are hundreds of other persons reading this book who are opening the door of their consciousness to Infinity, you can see that they also have access to the same Infinity, that Infinity to which Jesus had access when he said, "I and my Father are one." [2]

CREATION AS CONSCIOUSNESS REVEALING ITSELF

God is Spirit, and that Spirit is pouring Itself forth as your consciousness, taking form in the mind as your activity. You may be gripped with some great idea of beauty, and then within moments your hands begin to work with a pencil, a pen, or a brush, and this spiritual beauty that has entered your soul and is now expressing itself in your mind comes forth through your hands in tangible form. But it is the Spirit of God, which is now the Spirit of you, that has entered the mind as tangible form and comes forth as a concrete thing.

Every word that flows from the mind of God into your mind is what you live by because it takes form in the mind and then externalizes itself as what we call material form. Man must learn to listen for the still, small Voice until he actually receives inner divine guidance. Then he is led in one way or another through an idea in the mind and the work of his hands to the externalization of everything needful in his existence.

The Master tried very hard to teach his disciples and his listeners the spiritual nature of God and creation. He tried to make them understand that "man shall not live by bread alone, but by every word that proceedeth out of the mouth of God." [3] Why did the Master try to turn man away from depending on meat and bread? Why did he show him that he must not try to turn stones into food, even if he had the ability? Because that would make of man a creator, a supplier, and man is meant to live wholly in the consciousness of Spirit and let It perform Its miracle of Grace.

If you go beyond the material sense that urges you to be practical because you must have money, food, and clothing, you will begin to experience something wonderful. Free yourself from this material sense into which you were born: "No, no, no! Spiritually, I can grasp the fact that God is Spirit; and, therefore, my need is God or Spirit. Having God or Spirit, all these things will be added unto me. I will be practical with the end product of my labors: the money or the property that comes into my hands, the business or the profession that unfolds. I will be practical with it and not wasteful.

"But I will not be practical in believing that I myself am living in a material world and must do something of a material nature to bring about my own unfoldment of supply, of ideas, and of home. Of course, I will work, and perhaps harder than ever before, but it will be the impetus of the Spirit driving me.

"Morning, noon, and night there must be a turning within to the realization that I have access to the infinity of God, that God is Spirit and His Spirit floods me, His love, His grace, His peace. 'My peace I give unto you,' [4] and in this moment of contemplation I receive it. Having been fed by the word of God, I now go about whatever human tasks are given me to do today, not being concerned with what I may do next year but rather following out all instructions given me today."

As you begin to perceive this, the nature of your human life changes. Something begins to unfold in your consciousness that also broadens your experience and takes it out into new directions. Since God is infinite, unfoldment continues to take place increasingly. Even though the Spirit of the Lord God is upon you and you are ordained and are showing forth His grace in one way or another, it is never static. There are always progressive and advancing stages.

Eventually you will be lifted so high in consciousness that you are functioning virtually without the body. Everything is taking place in the Soul, in Consciousness, and the body is playing a lesser and lesser part. It will not surprise you one day when you step right out and discover that you are no longer walking the earth, but are now living in and out from Consciousness. Your friends and relatives will say, "He fell asleep." But that is not what has happened. Just as you outgrew your infant body, your body of youth, and your body of maturity, so eventually you will outgrow the entire human form, have no need for it, and then go on into the higher forms of life, where you operate behind the scenes.

AVAILABILITY OF ATTAINED SPIRITUAL CONSCIOUSNESS

Human beings left to themselves would just go on being human beings. There would be no such thing as progression. What they are today they would wake up and be tomorrow, and what they are tomorrow they would wake up and be the day after tomorrow. Year in and year out, they would go on living that materialistic sense of life. Fortunately, each one in some life-experience finds that his thought turns away from the pains and the pleasures of material sense, and he begins to seek something of a higher nature.

To each of us individually, there comes a time when this reaching out takes place, and I want you to know that behind this visible scene those who have attained the consciousness of a Moses, an Elijah, an Isaiah, a Jesus, a John, a Paul, or a Buddha still live. They have never died, nor have they ever let us die out of their consciousness. The same Spirit that prompted them to teach and to heal while on earth still animates them to heal and teach from their present elevation of consciousness, and they can reach us just as readily as they did when they were walking the earth. When they were here on earth, it would have been almost necessary for us to go to the land where they functioned to receive their grace. This is not necessary now because they have transcended the belief of time and space, which is another aspect of material sense.

As long as you live in material sense, you are limited. The wiser you become in how to live, how to eat, and how to keep the mind active, the longer you will live even humanly. But once you begin to open your consciousness to the Spirit of God, you will add still more years, and yet years should not be the criterion of life. The mere fact of living to eighty or ninety should not be considered of too great significance. First of all, unless those years are reached in health and harmony and with the full use of all faculties, not the way too many persons reach them, it is no achievement.

It is not necessarily years that determine the spiritual nature of life. Jesus was probably only thirty-three years of age when he made the transition, and most of his disciples did not reach any great age. So years cannot be the determining factor in how spiritual a person is. The determining factor is how rapidly he develops, how rapidly he matures spiritually, so that he can be done with this particular phase of experience and go on to whatever must be beyond.

FOR MOST PERSONS, DYING DOES NOT CHANGE CONSCIOUSNESS

Easter reminds you to turn your attention to the time beyond this earthly experience, not with a fear of it, not with a dread of it, and not even with grief and sorrow over those who leave this plane. Face this experience from the standpoint of resurrection and ascension. The truth is that you do not die; you are merely resurrected out of the tomb of mind and body and ascend into the realm of Soul-living, God-living, Consciousness-living.

By the act of dying, you do not become any better than you are now, or any worse. You remain the state of consciousness that you are now. Some evidence of the truth of this may be gleaned from experiments in the practice of spiritualism, that is, the ability to make contact with those who have gone on. The contacts that have been made of which we have any knowledge have been made with the same state of consciousness that those who have left this plane had before the transition. Whatever their interests were on earth so their interests remained. Therefore, if someone were to contact you after you had made the transition, you would probably respond in the same way as you would if you were visible as form. You would not have risen higher in consciousness or gone lower, except that those who are quite far along on the spiritual path would be advanced even further by the act of passing.

Those who have attained a measure of the fourth-dimensional consciousness, some measure of their masterhood here, like the masters of the world, go immediately into what is their original or native fourth-dimensional consciousness. No one could make contact with those on that spiritual level unless he himself had attained some measure of that level. Then he would be in contact with that consciousness.

What the world calls death is only setting the stage for ascending out of the materialistic sense of mind and body. I can conceive that a person could so rise in consciousness above the materialistic sense of time and material limitation as to live even in the flesh indefinitely, if there were any occasion for that experience. Why not? It is only a matter of understanding the nature of the body. However, if you believe that the seed is the beginning of man, then it is conceivable that you must believe that there is an end to that which has come forth from the material seed. But as you begin to perceive that Something preceded the seed, that the seed itself is an emanation of Something not material, the infinity of life is revealed.

34

Begin to see that God, functioning as individual consciousness, fills you with life, truth, love, grace, with a spirit of sharing, with even the spirit of communing. Then you will know why there is an attraction from man to woman and woman to man, each to find his own, and that all that follows is just the love that God has planted in their souls, taking form in mind and body and then bringing forth man in the image and likeness of God.

The parent should not only know this truth silently before conception, during pregnancy, and after birth, but then, as rapidly as the child can grasp it, lead the child to periods throughout the day of turning within to receive God's grace and protection.

As this experience is multiplied, gradually a whole new people will be brought forth on the face of the earth, a people no longer under the law, but under Grace. Then it will be revealed that man is on earth that God may be glorified, that His kingdom may be the earthly kingdom, and the earthly kingdom, His kingdom, for these must be one.

· 4 ·

The Operation of the
"Arm of Flesh"
and the Operation of Truth

THE RELIGIOUS LITERATURE AND FOLKLORE OF THE WORLD have a theme running through them which is not often understood and is sometimes taken lightly, a theme exemplified in statements such as these: "The Father that dwelleth in me, he doeth the works.[1] . . . I can do all things through Christ which strengtheneth me." [2] There is Something beyond human understanding which at some time or other plays a very great part in our experience and in the lives of the spiritually illumined. Accounts of something of a miraculous nature, always present in time of need, can be found in every mystical teaching.

Eventually religious teachings were built up that gave not only the promise of something Divine, but also of another presence, the devil, Satan, evil, the angel of death, so that there were good influences in the lives of those who were entitled to the good and evil influences in the experience of those who were deserving of some evil.

The idea of the supernatural is a dominant theme in mythological literature. In the mythology of Hawaii, there are the mena-hunes who are always out doing some good thing that the people humanly could not do for themselves. The Irish, too, have their

36

leprechauns. In folk literature, always this something or other that is a protective influence in the experience of the people is present.

In the opera *Parsifal* the entire cast of characters created by Richard Wagner exemplifies the awakening of the Soul. The story centers around the Soul-unfoldment of three men. One of these is Titurel, an old man who had lived a very good pure life as the keeper of the Holy Grail. He did his work nobly, protecting the Grail from theft and harm, and when he retired, his son, Amfortas, succeeded him. But the son was not as conscientious as his father, nor was he as pure, and the Holy Grail no longer served its noble purpose. Amfortas became involved with Kundry, a woman of questionable morals, and was drawn to evil companions, going from one unfortunate situation to another until the power given him as keeper of the Grail was taken over by his adversary, the wicked Klingsor, and Amfortas then suffered from a wound that would not heal. Into this situation came the pure Parsifal who withstood every temptation and was able to reveal the mystical Holy Grail once again to the knights. This is a brief and inadequate summary of the main theme.

It would seem that Parsifal, Titurel, and Amfortas were all important and different characters in this music drama. But what Wagner is telling us is that there is only one character in his entire opera, just one man. That man, Titurel, in his original state of purity, is the embodiment of the qualities of goodness, purity, and wholeness, but he also embodied within himself the potentiality of dropping from his pure estate to the ordinary human state of a mixture of good and evil. His falling from Grace shows forth as his own son, Amfortas, who, with his qualities of evil, is but another facet of Titurel's own nature. Parsifal, on the other hand, represents the return to man's pure state of divine sonship.

In the Bible, this same metamorphosis is represented as the first

Adam in the Garden of Eden and then the Adam who was cast out of the Garden of Eden because he did not maintain his purity. Moreover, in this allegory, Adam had two sons, Cain and Abel, who personified the qualities of good and evil inherent in man. Their struggle is typical of the age-old struggle every human being experiences on his way back to the Father's house. But there is only one character: Adam. The first Adam and the last Adam are the same Adam in different states of consciousness.

That is also the significance of the story of the Prodigal, the son of a king who wandered out on his own, sank to the lowest depths, and then in a moment of awakening returned to his father's house.

Our Consciousness Externalizes As Our World

In many different ways and different forms, there is brought home to us the lesson that we, in our own consciousness, embody the entire world, all its good and all its evil; and it outpictures as if it were a "you" and an "I," a "he" and a "she." Our experiences are all the externalization of the state of consciousness to which we have lent ourselves. A person may have begun life as the most promising of children, and yet in maturity become the most wicked person conceivable, but then he may be transformed from that state into the most upright of men.

The truth is that we are not in the world: the world is in us, and we are externalizing in our lives our own states of consciousness. We embody within ourselves the angel, the menahune, the Christ, the Spirit of God, but we also embody within ourselves the angel of death, forms of superstition, ignorance, and fear.

Jesus was by himself, alone, when suddenly the devil appeared before him. That was the appearance, but there was no devil there.

The devil was what was being projected out of his state of consciousness. He was not being tempted from outside: he was being tempted from within.

Witness an example of this today. Of the possibly one hundred thousand bank tellers in this country, probably only five of them are tempted by the money in front of them, whereas to none of the rest of them is this money even the suggestion of a temptation. That would indicate that it is not the money that tempts a person: the temptation is from within.

We always project the temptation so that it appears outside of us, and we say, "He tempted me"; "She tempted me"; "It tempted me." When you attain spiritual maturity, you realize how nonsensical that is. No thing and no one have the power to tempt any one of us except insofar as they are facets of whatever our own weakness may be. No one really has dominion in his life until he comes to an understanding of the truth that he embraces within his own consciousness all that he is to externalize in his experience.

No one can find anything any place that he does not bring there. If he is to find love, he must bring love. If he is to find friendship, he must bring friendship. If he is to find honesty, he must bring honesty. These qualities are not to be found in any place; they are not out in the air. Whatever qualities there are, they are to be found in consciousness—your consciousness and mine.

How true this is of success! There are some persons who get up at six o'clock in the morning and begin early so as to be on the job in order to achieve success. Others wait until eight or nine. But whether a person gets up at six or whether he gets up at nine, there is nothing outside of him to make him get up at either time. He is being prompted from within.

The Subliminal Activity of the Universal Mind

Each one of us embodies infinity in his consciousness. Unless we know this, we lay ourselves open to being the victims of thoughts or ideas that we pick up out of the atmosphere—actually not out of the atmosphere, but out of consciousness. This is plain when it is understood that *there is only one universal mind of man.* For example, the qualities that prompt Americans in their daily activities are the same qualities that prompt Englishmen, Germans, or Frenchmen. Humanly, we are all basically alike, not that every individual in this human experience is like every other individual, but every race or nationality is like every other race or nationality in that its people are prompted by the same basic motives because there is only one universal mind of man.

You and I can pick up anything that is in that universal mind and be influenced by it without knowing it. Subliminal advertising has given positive proof that there is one universal mind and that we can be influenced by it without even knowing that we are being influenced or that it is being projected at us.*

This is exactly what I mean by the influences that govern our human experience. A man is tempted to steal, and in his ignorance thinks that he is a thief, whereas the temptation is actually a projection of the universal mind. Another man is tempted sexually, and another one is tempted in some other way. But it is never the man himself. It is the subliminal activity of that universal mind projecting itself, to which a person responds without even knowing that he is being hypnotized.

*For a further discussion of this subject, see the author's "Break the Fetters That Bind You" in *The 1958 Infinite Way Letters* (London: L. N. Fowler and Co. Ltd., 1959).

In the case of subliminal advertising, the hypnotizing is being done by those individuals who are responsible for projecting it, but this of which I am speaking is not being projected from any personal standpoint or by any individual or group of individuals. It is an activity of the universal mind projecting itself, and you and I respond at whatever level our temptation may be.

The moment we perceive that there is a universal mind that is projecting traits or qualities such as envy, jealousy, malice, greed, lust, or false ambition, we can protect ourselves by turning it off in the same way that we would switch off our radio. We can disconnect ourselves from it in the recognition that it is the carnal mind.

Anyone who comes to the realization that the operation of this carnal mind of man is not a law and does not function as law begins to set himself free from its operation, and bit by bit the effects of its acceptance begin to disappear because an externalized condition is maintained by the belief that supports it. Remove the belief and there is no externalized condition. It is like a picture on a screen. Remove the film and there is no picture on the screen. Remove the picture from mind, that is, the picture of material law, and immediately the externalized picture begins to disappear. The moment we realize that from a human standpoint we are antennas for the universal human mind and then assume dominion by understanding that all these so-called laws that operate as law are not law, we begin to nullify them in our experience. Much healing work is accomplished just by nullifying the action of the carnal mind, by knowing its nothingness, not fighting it.

To fight the carnal mind is to acknowledge it as having the power of law, but in our recognition of the fact that the only power that has law is that which comes from the Infinite, we are functioning from quite a different base. Nobody has ever been able to

41

nullify the law of love; nobody has ever been able to nullify the law of truth; nobody has ever been able to nullify the law of life. These continue because they have their basis in the Infinite, in Omnipresence, Omnipotence, and Omniscience.

Anything that has the law of Infinity behind it cannot be destroyed. We cannot alter or destroy truth no matter what kind of mental manipulation we engage in, and so, in proportion as we consciously nullify the effects of the universal carnal mind, we make ourselves subject to Infinity, to the divine Consciousness. Then we are the antenna, the outlet and the inlet, for good.

Hypnotism in and of Itself Is Not Power

When the Master spoke to Pilate, he was not speaking to a man: he was speaking to temporal power. Whether he was speaking in one moment to the temporal power appearing as Pilate or in the next moment to temporal power appearing as disease, sin, or lack, always it was, "Thou hast no power. What hinders you? Pick up thy bed and walk. Thou hast no power."

Temporal power does not have a law of God to sustain it. As long as we do not fight the evil, but are consciously aware of the truth that all evil is but subliminal hypnotism and that these subliminal perceptions are not and cannot be power, we can witness them dissolve before our very eyes.

We have all seen the power of hypnotism in a person who permits himself to be hypnotized, and we have also seen the powerlessness of it to operate on those who refuse to permit themselves to be hypnotized, which indicates that it is not hypnotism that is the power. It is the acceptance of it that gives it its power. But as long as we are abiding in the truth that that which is not of God is not power and that we ourselves are one with the

Infinite, we lift ourselves above the hypnotism of the senses.

"There shall no evil befall thee, neither shall any plague come nigh thy dwelling." [3] The world has been repeating this statement and succumbing to evil at the same time, not knowing that the statement was addressed to a "thee," to the "thee" that "dwelleth in the secret place of the most High." [4] He is the one who discovers that no evil comes nigh his dwelling place. He is the one against whom no weapon is formed—the one who dwells in this conscious realization:

"I and my Father are one." [5] *I am an inlet to, and an outlet for, the Infinite, the Divine, and none of these universal so-called laws is law. Therefore they are not operative in me, on me, or through me.*

I am neither an inlet to, nor an outlet for, the carnal mind. It has no law to maintain or sustain itself. It cannot operate in consciousness as law because I have perceived what the Master meant when he said, "Thou couldest have no power at all against me, except it were given thee from above." [6]

I am the inlet to, and the outlet for, the Divine, the Infinite.

It is just as much a responsibility, and far more important, for a person to make himself free of the universal carnal mind and to make himself consciously one with the Infinite as it is for a person to decide to be a success in life in whatever field he may choose.

Every one of us has a Something within him that enables him to rise above the limitations of his humanhood. It does take recognition of It. It takes stick-to-itiveness. And oftentimes after we have learned that It exists, we do not work hard enough to maintain It. But the fact of the matter is that we all have that Spirit in us. The major factor lies in the word "recognition." Sometime or other we must recognize that there is this Something within us,

Something not only greater than our human limitations, but Something great enough to lift us out of and above them. Then we must rely on It, learn to listen to It, learn to give It room in our consciousness to operate and to function.

THE CREATIVE INTELLIGENCE ORDAINED US FOR ITS PURPOSE

"Thou wilt keep him in perfect peace, whose mind is stayed on thee." [7] There must be the ability to keep the mind stayed on It: first, recognizing It, acknowledging It, and then holding fast to the truth that there is Something operating in our consciousness to bring us to our destiny. We should not try to outline what that destiny is or set a specific goal in the sense of wanting a certain job or a certain business. But we set the goal of attaining our destiny, whatever that may be.

An infinite Intelligence could not have created this marvelous universe without having created us greater than the universe and for some purpose greater than the fish in the sea, the birds in the air, the cattle on a thousand hills, or the crops in the ground. We are given dominion over all of these, and therefore, there must be locked up in us a destiny. The creative Intelligence must have ordained us for some specific purpose of Its own.

For the last six or seven thousand years of recorded history, however, man has lived, not under the law of God, not under the protective instinct of God, but more or less an animal life, a "creaturely" life. Life has been a matter of "dog eat dog," man eat animal, one animal eat another animal and so on. Somewhere, somehow, the pure man became the impure, as illustrated in the story of Parsifal. The son of God became the Prodigal. The immortal became the mortal. The Adam of the Garden of Eden became the Adam outside the Garden of Eden.

When it happened, where it happened, or even how it happened cannot be pinpointed. The fact is it did, and as a human race we have strayed from our Father's house. We have left the Garden of Eden, the one world of spiritual consciousness, and we have lived for all these centuries by our wits and our own power, misusing them more than using them rightly. Only now are we coming to the understanding that we can return to the Father's house by a specific way.

There must be a recognition that our humanhood has been a direct result of the subliminal action of the universal human mind, that which in The Infinite Way we call hypnotism, mesmerism, suggestion, or malpractice, not as from one individual to another, but out of the universal carnal mind. We thought we were the man of earth, somehow separate and apart from God, somehow lost and not knowing how to get back. But now we know our oneness with the Father and that we have merely lost our way because we have forgotten our identity. We have not consciously known who we are, what we are, and even where we are.

So throughout the day and night we go about our business performing what is given us to do, always recognizing that in addition to our own efforts, there is this Presence working in us, with us, and through us: *I* in the midst of thee am mighty.

· 5 ·

The World of Material Sense
and the World
of Spiritual Discernment

WHEN THE MASTER SAID, "My kingdom is not of this world," [1] he implied that there are two worlds. And yet the truth is that there is only one world. God made all that was made, and anything that God did not make was not made. Since God is Spirit, the only world is a spiritual world, and the only man is spiritual man.

Then what did the Master mean when he said that his kingdom was not of this world? And what do we mean when we speak of the two worlds as taught in The Infinite Way? First of all, we mean that there is only one world, and it is spiritual. The other world is the materialistic concept that we entertain of the spiritual world; it is not really a world any more than the world of the insane is a real world. The world of the insane is a world lived within the mind, an imaginary world they have conceived. It has no external existence, any more than does the materialistic concept of world that we all accept have an existence separate and apart from mind. The proof of that is that through the development of spiritual discernment we are able to see the world as it is, to see the materialistic concept evaporate and in its place behold a world of harmony.

The human being lives in a world of material sense, and this means that he measures life in terms of amounts, weights, and degrees. He ascribes power to germs: good power to some germs and evil power to others. He ascribes powers of good to some individuals and powers of evil to other individuals. He is always conferring power upon someone or something. His entire human experience is made up of a combination of good and evil; he gives power to all kinds of things external to himself. Practically everything good comes from someone else or something else, and practically everything evil comes from some other person or some other thing. He is either the beneficiary or the victim. Rarely does he acknowledge that he has dominion and live out from it.

As men and women turn from an orthodox teaching to a mystical one, they begin to reverse this, although they cling to many of their former concepts for a long time. Not only do they begin to give more power to God and less power to the external world, but they now give power to God *over* the external world. They turn to God as a power over disease, and practically all their prayers are for healing or for some form of well-being. Through this turning, gradually they begin to acknowledge that although evil has power, there is Something called God or Truth which under certain circumstances has power over the evils of this world.

So begins the search for God. During that search, these persons are living between the two worlds: the world of material sense in which they give power to persons, things, and conditions, and the world of spiritual awareness where they begin to believe there is Something greater than the external powers of evil. It is a volleying back and forth, living part of the time in the world of acknowledging the power of mind and matter and part of the time living in the world of accepting God as the greater power of the two.

MEDITATION IS THE WAY TO FREEDOM

Very few persons have been able to lift themselves above the two worlds because no one can do this unless he has a revelation within himself. Moses proved the nonpower of Pharaoh; Elijah proved the nonpower of his persecutors and the nonpower of lack and limitation; Jesus proved the nonpower of sin, disease, and death; but the realization of these saints, seers, prophets, and teachers does not free us.

The ultimate truth is that we can become free only by the word of God. To me, the word of God is the truth revealed within and coming forth from my lips; but to you, it is only a setting forth of the way in which you can be free. It cannot guarantee you your freedom. You may experience temporary health and temporary freedom, but this is not real freedom. Freedom can come only from God, and that can take place only as an activity within your own consciousness.

Some of our students have attained their realization of God, and through that their freedom, and they may have had the feeling that I did it for them, but I did not. It was the responsiveness in their consciousness. Surely, had I done it for one, I would have done it equally for everyone. It would be my greatest joy to see everyone free this minute, but I do not have that power. The grace of God operates in my consciousness, and then each student receives It in proportion to his own readiness. For this reason some students have tremendous experiences with their first meditation, and some not until five or ten years later. It is usually a gradual experience, because, without inner preparation, it is very difficult to receive truth in one glimpse. Moreover, the shock is so great that a gradual transition in consciousness must take place.

It was given to me that the way lay in those moments of meditation when I could be quiet and receptive to the still, small Voice. Then I knew that this was the way in which ultimately everyone who had sufficient patience to attain meditation could be set free.

I would like you to see what sometimes happens with sudden revelations. I had been giving a class in Victoria, B.C., Canada, and was on my way to California for another class. I took the plane to Seattle, and, while waiting in the Seattle airport to catch another plane, an idea struck me "out of the blue." It was so powerful that I immediately began to write a page and a half which I called "Between Two Worlds." That was twelve years ago. Each year I took out those pages and read them, but nothing further would come until yesterday morning on Maui* when the whole secret flooded me. Remember, this was after twelve years of waiting!

Meditation opens consciousness and prepares the way to receive truth in consciousness. The truth is that there is but one spiritual universe, the kingdom of God, which is the same on earth as it is in heaven. As human beings, however, we cannot behold heaven on earth until we have developed our spiritual faculties. If we are to behold heaven on earth, we must develop the spiritual faculty of discernment, which is something entirely different from any of the human faculties or physical senses, none of which can bear witness to truth.

Spiritual healing has to do with the faculty of spiritual discernment whereby an individual who has attained some measure of that capacity is enabled to see and to declare, "Thou art my beloved child in whom I am well pleased. No iniquity has touched

*March 28, 1964.

thy household, thy soul, mind, or body." Remember, the eyes contradict this, the ears, the nose, the taste, the touch—all these contradict spiritual sense. How foolish it would seem to one deep in material sense to be told, "You and the Father are one, and all that the Father has is yours. No weapon that is formed against you shall prosper." How absurd this is to a person who is witnessing all the weapons that have been formed against man and seeing how effectively they are operating!

The person who has risen to the place of dwelling in the higher consciousness is living in an entirely different world. There the weapons that are formed against him cannot prosper, and the evils that float around in the air cannot come nigh his dwelling place. But this applies only to those who abide in the Word.

THE GREAT TEMPTATION: ACCEPTING A MATERIAL UNIVERSE

In the human world, there is just one universal mind, and since everyone is attuned to that one mind, everyone receives impressions and impulses of both good and evil. Whatever is common to the one universal human mind is common to all of us. We are not only tempted by what the world calls sin: we are tempted by disease, by fear, and by lack, because this universal human mind is made up of the pairs of opposites: abundance and lack, health and disease, life and death, wealth and poverty and all the gradations between.

Until we learn better, there are temptations that come to us, just as they came to the Master. We hear about the "three temptations," but actually every experience Jesus went through during his ministry, whether it was an insane man, people who were hungry, or a withered tree, was a temptation. What manner of tempta-

50

tion? The temptation to judge by material sense.

What about Peter's mother-in-law who was old enough to die? Why not let her die peacefully? Yes, judging by material sense, but in his ascended consciousness, having seen God as the Father, Jesus knew there could not be a material person. In other words, the temptation to see an old woman had to be reinterpreted.

Material sense would convince us that we are individuals who are born at a certain time, begin to age at a certain time, and also begin to deteriorate in capacity at a certain time. But as we outgrow a material sense of life and think in terms of God as our Selfhood, we can stop taking anxious thought, turn our attention to whatever work has to be done today, and then behold all these other things in the external, appearing in due order.

In this period of living between two worlds, we are going to be called upon to face temptations, as on occasion we have been called upon to face tidal waves in Hawaii. In the material universe, a tidal wave is a destructive power. But is there a material universe, or does that tidal wave represent merely a material sense of universe? Is it not the truth that Consciousness is the only cause, the only law, and the only effect? Therefore, Consciousness must be the substance of the waves. And is there anything destructive in God's consciousness? Could the creative Principle of life have created anything destructive to Itself? We are living between two worlds, however, and there is enough material sense left in us to be tempted by the appearance of a tidal wave, but there must also be enough elevation of consciousness for us to be able to sit down and realize:

Am I accepting external powers? Am I accepting power in things? Or am I accepting the truth that all dominion is given unto me, and this means individual consciousness? If all power is in individual consciousness, then all power is good, and there is no power external to it.

We may be faced with an epidemic or with an election, and that is a temptation to believe there is a destructive or evil power in the infection, the contagion, or the election. But we must realize that no weapon that is formed against us can prosper, and it cannot, if we have learned not to take up the sword which is double-edged. And by that we mean that the sword we are pointing at our neighbor's throat has a reverse side which is pointed at our own.

"This world" is a mental world. The body cannot be sick without our accepting sickness in the mind. The body of itself certainly cannot sin; it cannot of itself steal or defraud. In fact, we cannot carry out anything physically without first accepting it in the mind. The world of mind is the material sense of world.

Then there is "My kingdom," the divine Consciousness, which is revealed by that mind that was in Christ Jesus. The attainment of that divine Consciousness is our goal, and once we have access to the divine Consciousness, we are experiencing less of the effects of the universal carnal mind of man and more of the fruitage of the mind of God. The ultimate in attainment is when we achieve full conscious union with the divine Consciousness.

There is a material sense of existence which is responsible for the ills or discords that come our way. We cannot look for a devil to blame. There isn't any. We cannot look for neighbors, enemies, or relatives to blame because even though the evil may appear in the form of one or more individuals, we never will be free of the discords and inharmonies of life while we are accepting appearances and believing that it is a person, group, or nation, that it is the ideology, weather, climate, infection, or contagion that is responsible for our ills. The ills are due only to one thing: to a material sense of existence.

To the extent that you and I are still troubled with problems, be assured that it is because some measure of material sense persists. We still entertain a material sense of body; we still entertain a material sense of volcanoes and earthquakes. None of these is material, for God created all that was made, and God is Spirit.

When we see structural or physical man, we are really seeing material sense. But there is no such thing as structural man. Man is that selfhood that is completely invisible to the eyesight. No one has ever seen man with his eyes. The moment we think in terms of sinful, diseased, or deformed man, we are merely permitting material sense to govern our thought and obscure our vision.

Spiritual Discernment Reveals Infinity

While we are living between two worlds, material sense says there is power in the body: power to be healthy, to be diseased, or to be sinful. But then we must draw ourselves up into a higher state of consciousness and realize that it is only material sense that is telling us this because in the Garden of Eden there is just pure being.

Material sense has hypnotized us into accepting the belief of threescore years and ten, a few more or a few less. But if we look out at this world with spiritual vision, do we see anything destructive to us or to our body? It is only our acceptance of an aging process, a deteriorating power, that makes us subject to it. Through our higher consciousness, we know that there is no influence out here affecting us, so we are not affected by the thoughts, opinions, and concepts that are floating around in the air. We will not prove this, however, except in proportion as we open our consciousness several times a day to the realization that our consciousness has access to Infinity, and Infinity is flowing in us and through us and as us *now*. We are then building a consciousness in which we discover that man really does live by every word of truth that flows through his consciousness.

Material sense has to do with quantities and qualities, but spiritual discernment has no awareness of quantities or qualities— not even large quantities, not even good qualities. Spiritual discernment knows only the allness of invisible Spirit. It sees God as the consciousness of individual being. It does not see persons as persons with qualities and limitations of their own. Spiritual discernment sees God appearing as individual being and realizes that every individual has the grace of God. Judging by appearances, this may not seem to be true, but let us always remember that what we see, hear, taste, touch, and smell represents the material and limited sense of things. What we discern inwardly will always be closer to the truth.

If we would benefit the world, we must forget praying about peace on earth, about victory over the enemy, victory for our way of life over another mode of life, or victory for our favorite political party. If we would be helpful to the world, we must look through appearances with the power of spiritual discernment and behold God's creation and God's government of man and of the earth, including the weather and the climate.

Living with the truth that has been revealed to us of the nature of what the world calls the material world—which revelation has shown us is not a material world at all—helps us along the way. The mystery is not how a material world came about, but rather the discovery that it never did. There never has been a second creation. What is called the second creation is really the illusory creation of the five physical senses that sees the horizon where there is no horizon, that sees car tracks coming together where they do not come together, that sees weather as sometimes destructive, that sees germs as sometimes harmful, that sees persons as sometimes dangerous. This material sense constitutes the unreal or illusory world. But there is no unreal or illusory world; there is a *sense* of evil, but there is no evil.

The world of material sense builds the human identity and then begins to take anxious thought for its life, health, supply, home, and companionship. The world of spiritual discernment realizes, "Son, thou art ever with me, and all that I have is thine," [2] and then with no anxious thought fulfills whatever work is given to be done each hour of the day and beholds the invisible Presence that goes before to "make the crooked places straight." [3]

The two worlds are the real world of God's creating with God expressing as individual being, your being and mine, friend and foe; and the other world, which is not a world, is material sense forming its own illusory concepts about the world and then making us act like squirrels in a cage.

Material sense imprisons us in our mind, whereas spiritual perception enables us to open consciousness to see with God's wisdom. Material sense builds a structural universe where there is no structural universe. The concept of good and bad weather and harmful and healthy climates is a product of material sense, just as the germ theory and the idea of wealth and poverty are concepts of material sense. As we think in those terms, we are in "this world." The moment we begin to recognize that God is Spirit, we are then perceiving with spiritual discernment, with our spiritual faculties.

Spiritual Discernment Reveals That Which Is

Just as intelligence enables us to ride without fear on a train because we know that the tracks do not come together in the distance, just as it is now possible to take a ship beyond the horizon because we have learned that there is no horizon in spite of appearances; so as our spiritual faculties are enlarged, enriched, and deepened, we will discover that every aspect of limitation begins to disappear. There is a greater and greater awareness of the fact that the five physical senses do not testify truthfully. Gradually, as we learn not to judge by appearances, but are still for a moment and let the Spirit of God bear witness, we will discern spiritually and we will see as God sees.

Any time that we are confronted with appearances that we do not understand, we must stop for a moment, pause, close our eyes, if possible, and be receptive as if we were listening. Then, in place of the sick or the sinning person, we will hear the Voice say, " 'This is my beloved Son, in whom I am well pleased.' [4] Neither do I condemn him," and neither will we.

The ability to move from the world of material sense into the world of spiritual discernment is proportionate to our ability to close our eyes to the appearance and wait for that inner intuition, the voice of God, to reveal to us the truth of what we are beholding.

It is as simple as that, and it is as difficult as that: difficult because we have been born and brought up with the idea of looking right at the appearance and then with our so-called human cleverness calling it good or evil and congratulating ourselves on what expert psychologists we are.

In facing the temptation that there is an external power, let us go back instantly and realize that Consciousness is the basic substance, cause, and law of all creation. All creation manifests the qualities, character, and nature of Consciousness. Spiritual discernment demands that instead of judging and arriving at an opinion, we close our eyes to the appearance, open our ears, and let God bear witness with our spirit. Then the spiritual truth behind the appearance will be made evident to us.

· 6 ·

Making the Transition From
Personal Sense
to Spiritual Being

IN THE WORLD OF "THE NATURAL MAN," [1] the human being who is not under the law of God, there is the personal sense of "I" which constitutes humanhood. You call me Joel, but I call myself "I." The "I" that I call Joel claims to have a mind of his own that forms opinions and concepts based on background, family, race, religion, politics, and education. Because of this human "I," Joel does not see or hear correctly. As a result the human sense of "I" looks out at you and, instead of knowing you as you are, immediately forms concepts, opinions, and judgments of you. If I were to tell you what my concept of you is, you would say, "Oh, that's not I. You don't know me. I am not like that at all."

If I could talk to the politicians I do not like and tell them how I see them, they would also say, "I'm not like that at all. My own mother would disown me if I were like that." Yet that is how I see them. You do exactly the same thing in your humanhood as you look out at your friends, your relatives, or your enemies. You are forming concepts and opinions of them, believing that they are like that. And they are not that way at all.

To each of you, a time must come when you set aside your views, opinions, and concepts, and turn within to let the Spirit bear witness with your spirit. As long as you judge by appearances, as long as you see and believe in good and evil, you are not under the law of God. Surprising as that may sound, you may as well accept it.

SPIRITUAL BEING FORMS NO JUDGMENTS

When you make the transition to the man who lives "by every word that proceedeth out of the mouth of God," [2] you form no judgments, but rather create a vacuum within yourself, resulting in an attitude of listening so that divine judgment can be rendered. Then you will discover that you never hear or see good or evil, but rather that the man and the universe of God's creating are revealed to you, and you see the people about whom you had entertained judgments of one kind or another in an entirely different light.

It is not that you have been seeing many things and many people as evil and are now beginning to declare that they are all good. That is nonsense. You are not to call the human scene good any more than you are to call it evil. That is the mistake made by metaphysicians who say, "I am spiritual"; "You are spiritual"; or "He is spiritual"; when all the time they should know better because, even though they may not be able to read the thoughts of others, at least they can read their own. You do not change in an instant from seeing everything evil to seeing everything good. No, you stop declaring persons or things as either good or evil and allow the judgment to be rendered within you. Then it will be neither good nor evil, but spiritual.

The word "I" is the devil, the I that I call Joel and the I that you call "I," the I that is formed by prenatal, family, and environmental influences. But at a certain period of your spiritual unfoldment something happens, and you are lifted out of or above the sense of "I." You find that that "I," which has been forming judgments, opinions, and concepts, is no longer there and is no longer operating. Of course, it does operate to a certain extent. Perhaps you still like the same food that you did before or have the same taste in homes or automobiles, but aside from that there is a great absence of that little "I." You are beginning to see without having formed a concept, opinion, or theory.

When this transition in consciousness takes place and the personal "I" is absent, you can hear about germs, infection, and contagion, or you can hear about your enemies without reacting to them, because now there is no "I" entertaining a belief about them, a concept or opinion. The words "germs," "infection," "tidal wave," "war," and "bombs" no longer fill you with terror, and the reason they no longer have that power over you is because there is no "I" there.

Fear is always brought about by the consciousness of a personal "I": I do not want to be sick; I do not want to die; I do not want to be enslaved; I do not want to be limited. Because of this personal "I"–consciousness, the moment anything is mentioned that is in any sense destructive to "I," this little "I" begins to protect itself; "I" begins to fear; "I" begins to seek for remedies.

When you make the transition to spiritual consciousness, however, you discover that there is no "I" that needs protecting, healing, redeeming, or saving. In short, there is no more "I"; there is no more personal sense of self because now the vision of *I AM* as God is revealed. There is but one infinite Selfhood, one divine *I*, one infinite Being, and I am That. Whether I call myself Joel or whether I call myself by any other name, I am still *I*, and in that awareness, there is no need of a God to fear, a God to sacrifice to, or a God to worship. The only God there is, is that infinite

Consciousness which is the intelligence, the substance, and the law of all creation: human, animal, vegetable, and mineral. There is one infinite divine Being which manifests Itself as your individual being and mine.

THE INDESTRUCTIBLE RELATIONSHIP OF FATHER AND SON

In the world of Consciousness, we no longer have opinions and concepts: we have vision, a vision that announces itself. I do not declare it, but *I* declares it. I do not think it: It declares itself, and It says, "Knowest thou not that *I*, God, am ever with thee. *I*, God, will never leave thee or forsake thee. *I* am come that thou might have life and life more abundant."

As this impartation flows in us and through us, we realize that this is not being said to us alone. This is God speaking to his beloved son, which I am, which you are, which he is, which she is, which it is. The Voice is not speaking to Jew or Gentile; It is not speaking to Americans or citizens of other countries; It is not speaking to white or black. It is speaking universally to the beloved son, which I am and which you are. A relationship is thus revealed between God, the Father, and God, the son, a universal divine relationship which never began and will never end.

As human beings there are no errors and no sins we can commit that can separate us from the love and the life of God. There is no degree of youth or age, of life or death, that can separate us from that Love and Life. For now, I—Joel, James, Robert, Mary, Mildred—and my Father are in the relationship of oneness, indivisible, indestructible, timeless, since "before Abraham was" [3] unto the end of the world.

In the world of "the natural man," in order to save my own life, I might want to destroy the life of whomever at the moment I considered to be an enemy. But in this other world where we recognize that *I*, the Father, and I, the son, are one, we also recognize that *I*, the Father, is the *I* of every individual. The *I* which I am is as indestructible as God; and, therefore, there would not even be the desire to save one's self, for the *I* of me and the *I* of God are one, not two—just one. Knowing this principle, the Master could say, "Greater love hath no man than this, that a man lay down his life for his friends." [4] Let us not forget, however, that the friend is also the brother and sister, and the friend is also the enemy.

Enmity can exist only when there is a personal sense of "I," and that personal sense of "I" can exist only while we are that sense of "I" that beholds good powers and evil powers. In the world of the higher consciousness, *I*, God, is the substance of all form; and therefore, there is no destructive form. There is but one world, one universe, one Consciousness appearing and manifesting as individual you and me.

In the world of "the natural man," there is abundance and lack. Both are based on the belief of a personal selfhood, "I": I have or I have not. The moment we have transcended that personal sense of "I," we discover that "the earth is the Lord's, and the fulness thereof." [5] That statement completely eliminates "my" abundance or "my" lack because I of myself neither have nor have not. When we have yielded up both our abundance and our lack, then the Father says to the son: "Son . . . all that I"—the Father —"have is thine." [6] There is no more abundance or lack: there is only allness, infinity, completeness.

It is the same with our loves and hates, our likes and dislikes. When the personal sense of selfhood has been overcome, we neither love nor hate, like nor dislike, but the wisdom and the love of the Father that are expressed as the son flow freely back and

62

forth between us. Just as it is the love of the Father that flows freely between the Father and the son, so it is the love of God that flows as the love between the men and women of the world—not my love, not your love, but the love of the Father manifested as the love of the son. Therefore, it is God's love flowing between us.

The infinite nature of God's love eliminates hate, envy, jealousy, prejudice, malice, and fear. We overcome hate, dislike, distrust, fear, animosity, and jealousy as we "die" to a personal sense of ourselves or of others. By rising into the higher consciousness, we recognize that the Selfhood of me is the Selfhood of thee, the Selfhood of thee is the Selfhood of me, and we are one in our divine sonship with God. This wipes out that man who eventually must be overcome by dying daily to personal sense in order to be reborn of the Spirit.

We are dying to the personal sense of self and we are being reborn each time we can acknowledge that "the earth is the Lord's, and the fulness thereof." Each time we acknowledge that *I*, the Father, and I, the son, are one, and are able to look out upon all mankind in the same way, we are dying to "man, whose breath is in his nostrils," [7] and we are being reborn of the Spirit. As we abide consciously in communion with our divine Selfhood, all that the Father has clothes, feeds, and houses us, governs, maintains, and sustains us.

I have no problems to overcome, no animosity, no jealousy. No weapon formed against God can prosper, and, as I and the Father are one, I, too, can know that no weapon that is formed against me can prosper. "The earth is the Lord's, and the fulness thereof," and the Lord is this I *in the midst of me, this* I *that is the health of my countenance, my fortress, my high tower. I need no external reliance and I need have no fear of anything external while I am abiding in the* I *in the midst of me, and while I am consciously letting the* I *in the midst of me abide in me.*

This is the prayer of the recognition of the relationship between *I*, the Father, and I, the son. We have no personal opinions because now the *I* that we are sees truly, sees no presence or power apart from God, hears no evil, knows no evil, and recognizes God, the divine Consciousness, as the Selfhood of all being. The recognition, the realization, and the acknowledgment of our spiritual identity bring the spiritual grace of God to individual experience, as we surrender the personal sense of man rather than trying to bring God's grace to the personal sense of man.

THE DEATH OF PERSONAL SENSE MUST PRECEDE THE RESURRECTION

All attempts to benefit "the natural man" by spiritual means must fail. Spiritual healing does not mean trying to bring the power of God to a human being; it does not mean trying to bring the infinite riches of God to a poor mortal; it does not mean making of God an employment agency or a marriage counselor. It means giving up the personal sense of self and letting it "die" rather than trying to bring God's grace to it; it means that the son of man must "die," so that the son of God can be raised up in place of that son of man, and out of that "death" a resurrection can take place. Then we no longer have material health or material wealth: we have spiritual grace, and we discover that it is literally true that God's grace is our sufficiency.

We hasten the day of our death to personal sense and our resurrection to our divine sonship as we consciously remember not

64

to judge by appearances, by what we see, hear, taste, touch, and smell, but that we are to be still and let this inner wisdom reveal to us what is before us. Then in that moment of silence when all judgment ceases, the inner wisdom says, "This is My beloved child in whom *I* am well pleased. This is thy brother, this is thy sister. This is thy Selfhood in another form."

The moment judgment enters thought, remember that word *I*, and smile to yourself. You have momentarily allowed the personal sense of "I" to come in, but then, as you pause for a moment, the real *I* that you are takes over and reveals truth. If you have been fearing germs, infection, contagion, storms, waves, or bombs, then wisdom reveals that "the earth is the Lord's, and the fulness thereof." So what have you to fear? Is there any evil on the earth?

When we see and hear with spiritual discernment, we find beauty and harmony in our family, community, national, and international life. "This is my beloved son": white or black, stupid or wise. Such distinctions are only differences created out of the ignorance of believing that there is a selfhood, an I, apart from God. To the personal sense of "I," we will say, "Be still. 'Be still, and know that I am God,' [8] " and then listen to the judgment of God that is uttered within and thereby behold the universe as it is in the image of God.

Through spiritual discernment, we can see as we would like to be seen; we can know as we would like to be known. We will then be able to understand why the Master could say: "Father, forgive them; for they know not what they do," [9] and we can see that they were being handled by the personal sense of "I": self-preservation and the desire for self-glory.

Our experience is determined by whether we are living through personal sense or whether we are developing spiritual discernment. The world of "the natural man" is the world of human judgments based on appearances and the conditioned mind. The other world is the world that is revealed to us when we no longer form any judgments.

We are constantly living between two worlds: the world of appearances and the world of spiritual recognition and awareness. By dedication and devotion, more and more of spiritual Grace and more and more of the spiritual Robe descend upon us and wholly envelop us.

· 7 ·

The Consciousness
of Omnipresence

WHEN WE COME TO A CERTAIN PLACE in our spiritual development, we wonder how there could be such a God as has been
worshiped in the last four thousand years, whether the Hebrew
God, the Christian God, or the Buddhist God. Through prayers
to that God, wars have not been wiped out, nor has peace been
brought to earth. Furthermore, whatever of longevity has been
demonstrated in this last half century has come by way of the
increased knowledge *materia medica* has attained through re-
search, resulting in a better understanding of nutrition and sanita-
tion.

Today many ministers are willing to admit that a new concept
of God must be presented to the people, because what has heretofore been presented has not been God but merely an image, and
a false one at that. It is not easy to come to a place in consciousness
where we are willing to acknowledge this and then ask ourselves,
"What is God?" The question is: *What* is God, not *who,* because
to think of God as *who* would be to substitute one false image for
another.

Think for a moment of Omnipresence, a Presence filling all
space, a Presence right where we are, whether we make our bed

in heaven, in hell, or whether we "walk through the valley of the shadow of death." [1] What is that Presence that is Omnipresence and at the same time All-power and All-wisdom? What is It? What is this Presence that is always with us, whose pleasure it is to give us the kingdom, this Presence that knows our needs even before we do, that which goes before us to make our way straight, that which prepares mansions for us? What is It?

As we turn these questions over and over in our mind without fear that there is any God that is going to punish us for such questioning, as we divest ourselves of faith in that which has never warranted our faith, we find that that Presence has not done all those things for us because we have not understood what It is and how It functions.

We must empty out the vessel filled with all these false beliefs and faiths and images in order that we may be filled with truth. It is true that in all ages there have been some few who have attained the wisdom, the understanding, and the actual demonstration of Omnipresence. But has the world shown forth any evidence of a divine Presence, an infinite power of good?

The inevitable negative answer to that question could be quite shattering to one's faith. Nevertheless, just because the false gods of this world have failed the world or because the people of the world have failed the one God, let us not make the mistake of the atheists and believe there is no God. Let us rather acknowledge that we have not sufficiently searched, but have accepted without questioning the beliefs, opinions, and theories that have been handed down to us.

If freedom has any meaning at all, its most vital meaning must be the freedom to think, the freedom to seek, to question, and to discover that which is beyond the horizon of accepted knowledge until we arrive at the goal we are seeking, a goal which is life harmonious, life abundant, life eternal.

Why should we deny that individually that is our goal? Why not be truthful and acknowledge that we are at this point in our study of spiritual wisdom but for one purpose, and that is to seek life eternal, to seek that which will bring peace on earth to all men throughout all time and ensure freedom so that freedom never again can be at the mercy of man? Why not acknowledge that our great hope is that that which is setting us free individually will prove to be what ultimately will embrace the entire world and set it free?

When one person attains spiritual freedom, he attains it for the entire world, even though it may take a century for the demonstration on earth of the fullness and fulfillment of this freedom. It should be the goal of every individual who has been turned by the grace of God to the spiritual path, therefore, to seek and to search until he arrives, because if only one of us accomplishes this, it will set in motion that which will free the entire world.

Freedom Comes Through Conscious Oneness With Our Source

When a person is bound by some sense of limitation and turns to a spiritual practitioner for help, the help he gets is the realization on the part of the practitioner that God constitutes individual consciousness and that even the body is the temple of the living God. This sets the person free from the universal belief that he is mortal man with a mortal body. Since this is demonstrably true for one person, can we not see that one individual, or two or more gathered together, or "ten" [2] righteous men—only ten—knowing that God constitutes the consciousness of individual man, could set this entire world free? The only bondage there is, is the belief that we are insignificant mortal man.

Freedom will come with the understanding of God as Consciousness, of Consciousness as Omnipresence, and the realization that this Consciousness is the consciousness of individual man. Let us never think that freedom will come while we believe that God is anywhere except omnipresent as the consciousness of individual man. Freedom comes when we realize our true identity.

One individual discovering the secret of Omnipresence can release the world from its bondage to the limitations of material sense. But what is this Omnipresence that is present where we are, whether we are comfortably situated or whether we may at the moment be in some hell of sin, false appetite, disease, age, or even death? What is It that can set us free and, in setting us free, release all mankind from the slavery of bondage to the five physical senses and the limitations of the human mind? Consciousness is the creative source, presence, power, law, and cause, and only when we understand the meaning of Consciousness do we have the entire secret of life.

Consciousness Is the Source and Substance of Life

Spiritually there is no way to demonstrate permanent or lasting supply for anyone, because regardless of how much money a person may get, it is not supply. Even the largest amount of money may dwindle. But if we can bring a consciousness of supply to an individual, then he will never lack. We cannot even have health without first having a consciousness of health. That is why our work in The Infinite Way is not demonstrating health for a person, but rather demonstrating the consciousness of health for him.

I once asked a medical man what makes it possible for us to stand erect on our feet. His answer was, "Our muscles."

"What becomes of our muscles when we faint, when we become unconscious, or when we die? Does the body lose its muscles?"

"No, it still has muscles."

"Then why can we not stand erect? We have the same muscles when we fall asleep, the same muscles when we are unconscious."

The theory that muscles give us the capacity to stand erect is a satisfactory answer to those accepting a purely materialistic concept of the universe. It is true that from a material point of view, we do stand because of our muscles. The firmer and the harder our muscles, the longer we are able to stand, but once we have touched that higher realm of consciousness, we discover that it is not the muscles that keep us erect: it is consciousness. Consciousness enables us to stand erect, using the muscles as instruments.

So it is that there is nothing in the throat or mouth that can speak. A person may have all that is therein and yet not have speech because the muscles of the mouth, throat, and lips cannot move. It is consciousness using these instruments that makes them function.

Learning how to drive an automobile does not make one a good driver, as is proved by the fact that more people are killed each year by automobiles than by wars. Not everyone who can shift gears, put his foot on the gas pedal, start, stop, and park a car is a good driver. A good driver is one who has the consciousness which governs the mind, the thought, and the reflexes of the body that are important in driving. Without that consciousness, there is within every would-be driver the potentiality of what happens on our highways.

If we could count the number of bankruptcies that occur in

every year, we would know how easy it is to go into business and also how difficult it is to remain in business. It takes more than a sum of money to be a businessman: it takes consciousness.

The highest form of Consciousness, pure Consciousness, is Spirit. To understand Consciousness will enable us to understand the nature of Omnipresence because it is Consciousness that is Omnipresence. With the first glimpse of the meaning of Omnipresence, there dawns in thought the truth that whatever Omnipresence is, It formed the universe. There is a certain relative relationship between water and land, and probably there is some reason for this. The stars and planets move in fixed orbits, and there must be a reason for that, too. The Omnipresence that formed the universe must be a divine and infinite Intelligence.

As we look at the human body, we see evidence of that Intelligence at work. No person planned the body with its organs—heart, liver, lungs, brain—with its blood and nervous systems. No human being thought that up; no human being laid that out on a planning board. There must be an Intelligence that formed the human body, a creative power, law, substance, and activity, operating with the precision of an inexorable plan. Prayer, which to material sense would seek to have God help us on our way and perform our will, now becomes a communion:

"Not my will, but thine, be done." [3] *Thou performest that which Thou hast appointed for me to do. I cannot, therefore, seek Thy help for my way, but I can seek Thy help to establish Thy way in and through me. Let me be the instrument for Thy will, for Thy purpose. Thou dost not perform my will: Thou performest that which Thou givest me to do.*

We cannot pray to become at-one with God because always and forever we are one with the Father. That was the divine plan in

72

the beginning, and that oneness is already established, but until we are *consciously* one, the relationship of oneness is not functioning for us. To become consciously one means to surrender personal will.

MATERIAL SENSE IS A SENSE OF SEPARATION FROM CONSCIOUSNESS

To our knowledge, the sun, moon, and stars cannot think, and that may be why they are always under the government of God. We, on the other hand, think our way into a sense of separation. Notice that word "sense." We never really become separated from God in life or in death, but, through taking thought, we have built up a *sense* of separation from God which acts the same as if it were an actual separation.

Life began before conception, before birth, and life will continue after the grave unto eternity. "I will never leave thee, nor forsake thee.[4] . . . Lo, I am with you alway, even unto the end of the world." [5] There is no such thing as the end of the spiritual world because as long as there is Consciousness, Consciousness will be expressed. There can be no such thing as unexpressed Consciousness, for that would mean unconsciousness. Therefore, as long as there is Consciousness, Consciousness will be expressing Itself as the world and as men and women, but It will always be that infinite divine Consciousness expressing Itself individually.

Here again we are confronted with the two worlds: the world of pure Consciousness and the world of material sense. All who live in material sense know fear. There are no heroes in the sense of persons who do not know fear, but there are heroes who perform great deeds in spite of their fears. Fear is undoubtedly the major factor in governing the life that is lived in the five senses. We fear death; we fear accidents; we fear war; we fear poverty; we fear sickness; we fear the results of sin; and we certainly fear the calendar that is marking off the years. Fear! Fear! Fear! And freedom from that all-consuming fear can come only through the prayer of the recognition of oneness.

As long as we are consciously one with the Father, living in a receptivity to the spiritual impulse, we have nothing to fear. Regardless of what human situation or condition may arise as a temporary experience, we will have no fear because we are living in Omnipresence, knowing that since we have no will of our own, we have no doubt that Infinity can perform Its plan through us.

There seem to be two worlds, but actually there is only one: the world of Consciousness or Spirit. But there is a false sense of that one world which we entertain, and that false sense constitutes the other world, the world of material sense.

It is material sense that foists upon us the belief that we are body, made up of flesh and bone. Through spiritual awareness, however, the conviction comes, "This body is not I. This body is a handful of water and salt and minerals. I am not in the body; there is an *I* separate and apart from my body which is the owner of this body, and, therefore, the body in and of itself is nothing. I am the law unto it." If we believe there is life and intelligence in the body, in the water, salt, and minerals, we will reap what we have sown, which is the belief in material sense.

Scientists have said that the substance of matter is mind. However, the mind is still the world of the five physical senses, and it is only when we go beyond the mind that we are in the real world. While we are in the realm of mind, we can have a well body or a sick body, since mind and matter are one. We can have good or bad thoughts, material or spiritual thoughts, intelligent or ignorant thoughts.

Because Spirit is invisible Consciousness and has no qualities, we do not bring forth perfection unless we rise above the mind of good and evil into the realm of Consciousness where we find oneness. Spirit is Spirit. It just *is*. H_2O is neither good nor bad: it just *is*. Negative and positive electricity is neither good nor evil: it just *is*. Only our use of it can make it good or evil.

The world of material sense with its good and evil must be put off, but remember that no amount of studying and no amount of instruction will put it off. The only thing that will put it off is realization. When you take a truth into your consciousness and abide with it and let it abide in you until a moment of realization, you will have put off some measure of mortality.

In your meditations, close your eyes and take the word *I*, and then realize the invisible nature of your Self, of the *I* that you are. Realize that your body is visible, but *I* am not visible. Then remember these passages of Scripture: "I am come that they might have life, and that they might have it more abundantly.[6] . . . I am the way, the truth, and the life." [7]

Look at your body, your business, your marriage, or your home, and realize: "Of myself, I am nothing. This *I* that I am is the law and the substance; It is the food that feeds the body; It is the cement of the business, the marriage, the human relationship."

Sooner or later temptations in the form of lack may come, as they came to the Master. Suddenly the mind begins thinking of dollars, as the mind of Jesus turned to the thought of bread. But he quickly recognized the nature of the material sense which claimed that power was "out there" in bread. You, too, must jump up into that higher realm and say: "Man does not live by bread alone. Man lives by every word of God, by every spiritual impulse, received in consciousness."

Certainly the Word appears outwardly as bread, money, muscles, or the functioning of the body. The realization of *I* appears to bring forth fruitage on what we call the material plane, but it is not the material plane. Even body and money are the instruments of God. If you think of money, property, good will, or trade as the outer manifestation of Consciousness, then these things will have the quality and the quantity of Consciousness, which is infinite. If you see them as something separate and apart from Consciousness, they become worthless.

Train yourself to weigh what comes into your mind in the light of the two worlds: "Am I placing power in something or someone external to the *I* that I am? Am I placing confidence in good or bad powers or in fear? Am I relying on external power and believing in infection or in the calendar? Am I living in the world of material sense and material values?"

When such thoughts come to you, reinterpret them: "No, I do not live by bread or by property, but by the will of God. Life under God is not at the mercy of accidents, germs, or heredity. As I withdraw power from the external realm, as I 'die' to my humanness, I am reborn into my spiritual sonship." As you draw power back into the *I* that you are, fear of the outer world disappears.

Why outline what God's will or destiny should be for you? Instead let the inner ear be open as you listen with the invisible ear, waiting to hear the inaudible word of God. You are not asking for anything: you are realizing your oneness with your Source, communing with It, and making room for the Spirit of God to awaken in your consciousness. Then It will do Its work in you and for you and through you. Always It will do it.

76

· 8 ·

The Way to Fulfillment: Right Identification

ON THE SPIRITUAL PATH, the revelation and realization of right identity is of the greatest significance because it is through a realization of this principle that the entire world will eventually enter a new era of living.

Very few during their human span ever come to know their true identity or the identity of their friends and relatives. They are always living in a world of illusion like characters on a stage. Long ago Shakespeare wrote, "All the world's a stage, and all the men and women merely players." Our humanhood is a masquerade, and we are hiding behind our mask. Not only are we hiding from ourselves, but when we look at others, the mask they are wearing called personality is what we are seeing. We are judging them by what we see instead of realizing that behind the mask of personality and stage costumes is the real Self, or real identity, of the individual.

As we persist in judging one another by what we appear to be, we are all taking part in a great masquerade, looking on one as Romeo and another as Juliet, one as Hamlet and one as Satan, never noticing that behind the masquerade, there is an immortal being who was never born and will never die and who is an individual manifestation of the Divine. As long as life is lived through the mind and the body, it will be impossible to live the life of our real identity and share the joyous experience of communion with one another that comes once we have gone beyond the body and the mind of a person and reached the realm of his Soul.

Man is made up of three parts: Soul, mind, and body. The mind as a factor in healing has always been recognized by metaphysicians who have discovered that if they can bring the mind into some measure of wholeness, completeness, and peace, the health of the body automatically follows. But a higher factor, the Soul, must be taken into consideration because it is in the Soul that harmony is revealed and then established in the mind and the body.

If we wish to know ourselves, we will have to discover our Soul. If you wish to know me, do not believe you can ever know me by knowing how my mind functions or my body. You will have to commune with me in my Soul. There, I can reveal myself to you. When I want to know you, be assured that I do not enter into your mind or your body, but as I commune with your Soul, I realize we are both children of God, members of the one family of the household of God.

Right Identification

The understanding of our spiritual identity will solve all the problems of the world, because with right identification the principles of spiritual living will be revealed. These principles cannot be revealed, however, until we discover right identity and learn to commune with the Soul: your Soul and my Soul. It is within the Soul that the mysteries of life are hidden, and it is through the

Soul that they are revealed. We are living between two worlds, between the world of mind and body and the world of the Soul, and until we discover the realm of the Soul, we will not discover the secret of life.

When Pope Paul VI visited a prison on April 9, 1964, he said mass and gave communion to several hundred prisoners, telling them that he did not visit them out of any romantic or humanitarian reason, but because he saw in them the incarnation of the Christ. He made it clear to the prisoners there that man is not a sinner condemned to an eternal hell, but that even in the deepest degradation they could at any moment awaken to the realization of the full dignity of their manhood. To the newspapers this idea was not news. What was news to the reporters was that the Pope went to a prison, but that he told the prisoners that he witnessed the incarnation of Christ in man, even in a sinning man, they were unable to recognize as news of unprecedented significance.

Can you imagine what effect the Pope's words must have had on those prisoners? Do you know how impossible it is, once you know your true identity, once you have witnessed the incarnation of the Christ in man, to violate your mind or your body or the mind or body of your neighbor?

It is not given to any one of us to behold first the Christ of our own identity. That would be too intense an ego. So we behold It in someone other than ourselves, and then the light begins to dawn: God does not have just one Son. With that realization, the vision broadens, and suddenly we realize: "All those in whom I have perceived the Christ—Jesus, John, Paul, or Gautama the Buddha—were all men as I am until realization came, and then the Christ was made evident." That brings the Christ alive in us, and we can say, "Ah! I, too."

The Christ is incarnated in all men, not only in good mankind but evil mankind. What counts is: Does something within guide us to a person who can awaken It in us, lead us to a book or to a teaching? Then, although our sins are scarlet, we are restored. The real purpose of teachers, books, and teachings is to lead us back to the kingdom of God within ourselves so that we may be taught of God and our spiritual identity be revealed.

To be instructed by a teacher is right, and as it should be, but no one should spend his life sitting at his teacher's feet. A major problem in my work has been trying to avoid any kind of a dependent relationship between me and students who have come to me, or who have come to some of our teachers. Some of these students, believing that teachers are God-inspired, take the attitude of wanting to sit and partake of their light. That is good up to a certain point, but in The Infinite Way we are not trying to develop a following, nor are we trying to acquire fame or accumulate a fortune. I, at least, and some of the teachers who have been taught by me are trying—sometimes even against the pressure of students—to bring to them the awareness that students have just as much access to the kingdom of God as teachers have. If a person wants to do healing work, he can do as much as any one of us has done.

In The Infinite Way, the teacher acts as the instrument for the awakening of the student to the Christ-mind within him. Such work naturally appeals only to those students who wish to study, meditate, and receive ordination in their souls by the Spirit. Our teachers work with one student, with two, six, twelve, or a hundred —but not with masses. The masses are not yet ready to devote themselves to the hours necessary to attain "that mind" or to suffer the pain.

The Land of Milk and Honey or the Cross?

On the part of many, there is still the belief that in turning to the spiritual path they have discovered the land of milk and honey. There is such a land, yes, and they may be on the way to it, but it is going to be a long, long time before they are in it. True, some are a little ahead of others, but in their humanhood, they never can become good enough to enter the Promised Land. It is only when they "die" to their mortality that they can enter into their full Christhood.

It is one thing for me to acknowledge that the Christ is incarnated in you and for you to acknowledge that the Christ is incarnated in me. It is quite another thing to reach the place of realizing that there is no "you" and there is no "me": there is only Christhood. You are going to discover, as everyone has on this path, that there are some painful steps before you reach the Promised Land. The way to the crown is the cross, and there is no avoiding it. Problem after problem we overcome in ourselves and for our patients and students, until eventually we rise to where problems no longer enter consciousness because we have attained Christhood. But until that point, it is overcoming, overcoming, and overcoming, and overturning and overturning, "until he come whose right it is."[1] And that "He" is the Christ which is incarnated in us whether we be saints or sinners.

Until one overcomes good humanhood, he cannot enter Christhood because Christhood is a recognition of the truth: "There is none good but one, that is, God."[2] No one has entirely overcome humanhood during his earth span—not even the Master. In the Garden of Gethsemane, the Master still wanted to have the cup

81

pass from him; he still wanted his disciples to pray for him. That is humanhood. In Christhood, we do not need anyone to stay awake with us or pray for us because we do not have any cups to pass from us. As long as there is a trace of humanhood about us, we are going to find occasion for someone to pray for us, and we are going to be praying for certain cups to pass from our experience.

The Transition From This World to the Realm of Soul Is a Gradual One

Whoever attains the Spirit of God—saints and sinners alike—once the realization of his true identity, his Christhood is attained, even the first glimpse of It, begins to emerge from the world of material sense to the world of spiritual consciousness, from the world of mind and matter to the realm of the Soul. Those of us who have caught a glimpse of our Soul or the Soul of another, so that we realize that there is a realm of Soul in each one of us, can see what a different world we are living in than merely a world that is made up of climate and scenery, of health and sickness, or of wealth and poverty.

The higher we go in the realization of our Christ-identity, the greater the degree of inner unrest. Things and thoughts that were entirely natural to us when we lived wholly in the realm of mind and body are very distasteful when we touch the realm of Soul. Profanity and obscene stories grate on the ear and, although there is no sin in smoking and drinking except when there is an excessive indulgence in them, these things become offensive to us after we have been abiding for a while in the realm of the Soul. All the little trickeries and deceits of human life set up an inner conflict.

Entering the Soul-realm is not really a kind of hop, skip, and jump onto Cloud Nine and, from then on, having no awareness of the rest of the world about us. It is a gradual evolution out of this world into the world of Soul. Eventually, when we are far enough along in the realm of the Soul, these once distasteful things do not irritate us so much and sometimes do not even register in our consciousness.

Another difficult aspect of living in the two worlds is when we begin to witness man's inhumanity to man on a major scale. When some of the deep problems of our students and patients are forced upon our attention, we find ourselves reacting, but as we are able to rise and lift them above their problems, there come the moments of peace and happiness. Always the other moments have to be experienced, which probably will not take place when we attain full Christhood.

I doubt very much that Jesus Christ in his present consciousness would upset the table of the money-changers[3] or call anyone a "viper."[4] I doubt very much if he would even see or hear anything to bring forth such sentiments. Instead, as it hit upon his consciousness, it would be healed, dissolved, or removed. I am sure that when he came into the presence of the woman taken in adultery and the thief on the cross he felt no horror or disgust. He was not even aware of the presence of iniquity. It just touched his consciousness and was dissolved without bringing forth from him any resentment.

This must be true because I, too, feel the same lack of reaction to individual sin or sinners, and to poverty or disease. But I am affected by wickedness in high places. I am still moved by man's inhumanity to man on a national and international scale and to leaders who are betraying their trust and thereby harming whole populations. I still react to some of these things as the Master must have reacted to the evils he saw in high places. But I do know that he ascended beyond that and the day will come when I can and will.

Some day when we can behold the Christ in our Presidents, in our Congressmen, and in the dictators of the world, instead of seeing them as they appear to be, we will heal the world nationally and internationally. Probably you think that that is easy. But it isn't! And that is the cause of discord and inharmony within ourselves; that is why this path is not an easy one. It demands that we persist until the day comes when we can look right into the Soul of even those we consider the most wicked and there behold the incarnation of God. We can be assured that when there are those capable of this, there will be permanent peace on earth. Furthermore, the children of the coming generations will be born as the incarnation of the Christ because parents will conceive, not in moments of lust, but in moments of love.

SPIRITUAL FULFILLMENT IS THE GOAL OF THE WAY

We have to leave this world for that higher world. The space between the two worlds has been called the path or the way from material sense to Soul. We cannot enter the realm of Soul except through an activity of truth in our consciousness.

As right identification is the beginning of spiritual work, so the goal is spiritual fulfillment, that we may come into conscious union with God and a conscious awareness of our true identity. Even while we are working out specific problems, we remember that the solving of problems is not really our purpose in spiritual study and meditation. The goal is fulfillment: to be filled full of God, to be filled full of the Spirit, to have God-realization.

When we go to God, we must go for the gift of God—not for a perfect heart, liver, or lungs. And the gift of God is a spiritual impulse which takes form in the mind and then comes forth as a harmonious body. But if we do not receive that impulse, we will never have the form. The gift of God is not money; the gift of God is not an automobile or a house or property; the gift of God is nothing that partakes of a material nature: the gift of God is something of an incorporeal spiritual nature, and when we receive that gift, it translates itself into our experience as tangible form which may well be automobiles or houses or property.

A composer receives an impulse in the mind that takes the form of a melody, and then the melody comes out of the voice or the piano or the violin. Likewise the inventor receives an impulse which takes form as an idea, and he can then take the idea and mold it into a telephone or a wireless or anything else, but God cannot give the inventor a telephone or anything of a material nature. If we pray for the gift of God, the awareness of the presence of God, the mind interprets that awareness in the form of something tangible that can be shared.

Spiritual principles are the treasures we lay up in heaven. Human health or human wealth can disappear, but if we have the Spirit of God in us, It will restore "the years that the locust hath eaten."[5] Therefore, what difference does it make if we lose or give away all we have, as long as we have the Spirit of God which is the substance of it?

There is only one real reason why anyone has ever entered the spiritual path, and that is that he may be fulfilled, filled full of the Spirit of God. "In thy presence is fulness of joy." [6] Fullness! Could we have fullness of joy without health, abundance, good relationships, home? How otherwise could we be fulfilled? How could we be full of joy?

But when we are fulfilled, we discover that we are not fulfilled so that we may be happy, healthy, or prosperous. The reason we have been fulfilled is that we may share it. Anyone who has felt the Spirit of God upon him or been ordained of the Spirit has found his own fulfillment. One would think such a person could be happy, but he is not happy until he goes out and tries to teach it and preach it even if he ends up on the cross. No one who has received this can ever enjoy his fulfillment until he begins to share it.

What will happen when the world awakens to the fact that the Christ is incarnated in all men, rather than only in Jesus, and not only in all good men, but also in all sinners? What will happen when this world begins to understand why God's rain falls on the just and on the unjust? But it does fall on the just and on the unjust. Why? Because God is incarnated in man; God is manifest as man. He breathed His life into us, and it is His life in us which bears fruit richly as the health of our body, mind, home, business, or profession.

God is omnipresence and God is the same for all, but no one has God until he experiences It. Attaining the experience of God is the attainment of all the added things, with no asking and no telling. Through prayer and meditation, we have the power of coming into the presence of God, and in this Presence we are in the presence of fulfillment with all things added unto us.

· 9 ·

Becoming Instruments
of Grace
Through Reconciliation

OUR INDIVIDUAL FULFILLMENT comes about in proportion as we
become consciously one with our Source, and that oneness is
expressed in our relationship with one another. Since the one
Consciousness is the life of all being, we are automatically one
with all spiritual being, whether appearing as person, animal, vegetable, or mineral.

"If a man say, I love God, and hateth his brother, he is a liar:
for he that loveth not his brother whom he hath seen, how can
he love God whom he hath not seen?[1] . . . Inasmuch as ye have
done it unto one of the least of these my brethren, ye have done
it unto me." [2] In our service or devotion to man, we are expressing
our love for God and acknowledging the oneness of God and man,
and not only praying for ourselves and our friends, but praying for
our enemies and, thereby, making friends of the enemy.

Living in what the Master called "this world," [3] we are a state
of total limitation and believe that our lives are being maintained
and sustained by our own efforts or our own wisdom, not realizing
that we are a part of one another. Just as every branch is a part
of the trunk of the tree, so are we a part of the Vine, the Christ,
and that Vine, or Christ, is one with the Father.

Everyone on this earth is a contributing agency to the whole and, invisible to human sight, is the Vine that is the Christ, one with the Father, drawing unto himself individually all that the Father is and all that the Father has. We can relax and rest in the assurance of divine Grace because now we know that a Grace is operating universally, a Grace that begins with the Source and flows through our individual consciousness as through an invisible vine, maintaining and sustaining the Soul, mind, and body.

As human beings, we are like the Prodigal Son who separated himself from his father's house and began to use up his substance, none of which was being renewed. Only after it had all been used up did he realize what had happened and knew that once he was reconciled to his father and restored to his father's house, he would be heir to the entire kingdom.

So it is with us. The moment we become reconciled to, and at-one with, our Source, then, immediately we are heirs, "joint-heirs," [4] to all the heavenly riches. In my reconciliation, it is necessary to know not only that I am heir of God, but I must also know that I am joint-heir with you, so that I include you in that divine sonship. In my reconciliation with God *and* with you, I am fulfilled. In that state of reconciliation, we pass from the man of earth to that man who has his being in Christ. Now our ways on earth are prospered, not by virtue of ourselves but by virtue of our oneness with our Source and through that Source with all others.

ACCESS TO OMNISCIENCE AND DIVINE GRACE THROUGH THE TRANSCENDENTAL CONSCIOUSNESS

The man of earth, limited to his mind and to the strength of his body, lives at war with other persons, always seeking something that the other has, always wanting something that someone else has, always believing that the other person's grass is greener, and never realizing fulfillment within his own being. But as a transition in consciousness is made, he becomes aware of a transcendental Consciousness upon which he can draw.

Let us assume that we have lost some object—a ring, a pin, or any other possession—and we begin to rack our brain to remember what we could possibly have done with it. It may be, and often is the case, that eventually we find it again. But now, as we think of that lost object, we instantly remember that we have access to Omniscience, the All-knowing, and that we are not limited to our memory or dependent upon laborious searching. Rather we turn within, relax our conscious thinking, listen, and then are guided instantly to where the lost object is, or watch how it is returned to us. By what process? By the conscious contact we have made with the infinite Intelligence which governs and guides the universe and is the law unto this entire universe, and which we have now accepted as our intelligence, as the Source to which we turn. If that object is anywhere within our reach, we will be led to it; and if not, by patiently waiting and because we have Omniscience operating in and through our experience, it will in some way be restored to us. As long as we have Omnipotence and Omnipresence, we cannot miss.

In our business, professional, or family life, if we are aware of a lack, a discord, or an inharmony, instead of wondering what we can do about it, let us relax for a moment. Through our consciousness, we have access to the infinite All-knowing, which is ever-present and the only power, and we are immediately in touch with the necessary wisdom to bring about the solution. It makes no difference whether what claims to be present is physical illness, mental, moral, or financial illness, or an illness of human relationships, in the presence of God, it is dissolved and transmuted.

God has given us Its divine consciousness, and through our access to It, It becomes the bread, meat, wine, and water. Divine Grace can appear as our nets filled with fish even though a moment before the sea seemed to be empty of them. Divine Grace does not give us anything or manufacture anything for us: divine Grace appears *as.* It is never divine Grace sending something or giving something: it is divine Grace *forming Itself* as our daily need.

To move in consciousness from the man of earth who is entirely limited to himself—mentally, physically, and financially—to being that man who has his being in Christ, we must know this truth:

Divine Grace lives my life, and I live as a beholder of the glory of God on earth. It is the glory of God that appears as my Soul, mind, and body. It is the glory of God that appears as fruitage, harmony, success, and abundance in my life. Of my own self, separate and apart from that divine Grace, I am nothing, nothing more than a withering branch that is cut off from the tree.

But having been consciously reconciled to God and to man, I am now full and complete, living by the grace of God with access to all that God is and all that God has. All the good that is flowing in me, through me, and as me is the glory of God manifesting Itself. As I abide in this Spirit of God and let the Spirit of God abide in me, I recognize always that, although invisible, there is this transcendental Being within me to which I have access forever.

I am one with the Source, and in that oneness, I am one with the human, animal, vegetable, and mineral worlds, and the worlds beyond. I am at-one with the consciousness of every child of God who has ever existed from the beginning of time and with every child of God who will come into expression until the end of time.

I am in union with the divine Intelligence of the past, the present, and the future. No spiritual secret is hidden from me—not even those secrets that were known to the unknown Krishna of thousands of years ago and the secrets that will be known to the Buddhas and the Christs of ten thousand years from now, for we are united in the infinite divine Consciousness, which is the consciousness of all mankind on this planet and on every other planet where divine Consciousness functions.

This means omnipresence: omnipresence now, omnipresence of what we call the past and omnipresence of what we call the future. I am living in that omnipresence now. I am now in the consciousness of all who have ever lived, are living now, and ever will live in the divine Consciousness, for we are one. That infinite divine consciousness of God, the Consciousness of the past, the present, and the future, is my consciousness at this moment.

Oneness, a Universal Truth

Regardless of our present state of sin, disease, poverty, or enslavement, we have access to Infinity through our own consciousness because the Transcendental is present with us, and the realization of this truth must immediately begin to set us free.

As spiritual wisdom begins to reveal itself to us, it very quickly becomes apparent that this truth which has been revealed to us of our identity and of our access to Omnipresence, Omniscience, and Omnipotence must be a universal truth because it is impossible to personalize Infinity or Eternality. Thereby we are reconciled to one another and to all mankind. But if we leave one brother out of this spiritual family, we are disowning part of God's universe.

No truth that is revealed within us is ever for ourselves. It is always that God's grace may flow through us to those who may be led to us for light. Fruitage flows through us that we may share it with all who seek it. That is why every truth that is realized as a truth of our being must be shared with the entire world in silence and in secrecy, never breaking that silence or secrecy until we are called upon to do so. Silently and secretly, whenever a truth is revealed within us, we immediately open our consciousness and take in the world, and realize that this is the universal truth about all mankind, about the universe: the past universe, the present universe, and the universe still to come.

What a difference between the man of earth who has only his own mind and his own experience upon which to rely and that man who has access to the Christ-consciousness and the spiritual wisdom of the saints and sages of all time! Because we are reconciled to the divine Consciousness which is their individual consciousness, our consciousness, and the consciousness of those who will be uttering spiritual truth a thousand years from now, we have access to all their spiritual wisdom. The same Consciousness that will be expressing Itself through them is the Consciousness that is expressing Itself through us as we turn and live by Grace rather than by might and by power.

Back of every individual who has ever received a spiritual truth, an idea for an invention, or some kind of creative music or art, there is one infinite Consciousness which is its source. When a person taps that, he can tap all the wisdom proceeding from the one Source. The consciousness of individual man is infinite, and to bring forth infinity, all he need do is to turn within.

"My oneness with God constitutes my oneness with all spiritual being and with every spiritual idea or thing." * This oneness cannot be limited to time, space, or place. But it can come about

*Joel Goldsmith, *Conscious Union With God* (New York: The Julian Press, 1962), p. 230.

only through introspection, cogitation, contemplation, and meditation—through anything that takes the attention away from the outside world and draws it back to that Center within. Grace leads us to the realm of Consciousness within, and then an activity of Grace starts the flow:

Enter the sanctuary; close the door of the five physical senses; and listen to Me. *Seek* Me, *the infinite divine Being, and I will make you "fishers of men." No person can do it, but I will, that I that is the I of your inner being. I will show you the Way; I will go before you; I will prepare mansions for you. I will never leave you or forsake you.*

LIGHT-BEARERS

If we keep the principle that the divine Consciousness is our individual consciousness secret and sacred and if we practice it conscientiously, such miracles will take place in our lives as we ourselves could not believe possible. The way in which this works is a mystery to us, but because it sometimes appears in such natural ways, we do not realize that it is prompted by divine Grace. If we think of it in terms of God's grace, however, we will see how infinite it can be, not limited to us, but limited only to God's grace and to our receptivity. By our example, by our light, the world will see and seek that Light. And it will find It, because this is a universal truth.

The demonstration of Infinity in our experience is measured by the extent to which we practice a principle of this nature—never revealing it, never speaking of it, and never trying to teach it until we are so consciously one with it that it is flowing. Then we are the instruments through which the message comes. It blesses us, but its major blessing is that others are led to us, and it becomes a universal truth which blesses the entire universe.

This may cause a disruption in our life: a businessman may find less time for his business and a housewife less time for her home. More and more we discover that we are being drawn into a universal scheme of things. The Master—and I am not speaking of a man but of the Spirit of God within—says: "Follow me, and I will make you fishers of men," [5] and It pulls us out of our little fishing job into an activity that enables the Grace we have discovered to bless the world.

In the moment we prove that the infinite Consciousness of this universe is our individual consciousness and that we have access to the Consciousness which is, ever has been, and ever will be, we are called out as "fishers of men" to be a light unto the world. Light does not go out looking for places in which to shine. Like the sun which stays fast in the heavens, light shines and lets the rest of the world come to it. So, as we in some measure become the light, we hold what we have received sacred and secret until the world comes to our doorway for it.

The whole principle of the spiritual life is that we have access to Infinity through our consciousness, and then that we go within sufficiently often to let It flow, being careful never to personalize It and think we have become "good" or that we have become "spiritual." No, we have become instruments or transparencies for the infinite, universal Grace. We choke It and shut It off if we personalize It, but we can increase the flow by realizing It as infinite Grace flowing universally. This does not glorify us, but lets us stand still like the tree and show forth God's glory. Anything else is catering to the ego, and the ego must "die" as completely as the branch of the tree that thinks it is something of itself. So it is that this reconciles us to God and fulfills us.

94

What a wonderful thing to be reconciled to God and thereby to the wisdom of the ages! What a wonderful thing to be reconciled to God, Omnipresence, Omniscience, and abiding Grace! That Grace is our manna and since God's grace is omnipresent, our manna is present always, appearing as the form necessary to the particular moment. By God's grace, manna reaches us to give us our spiritual, mental, moral, physical, and financial freedom: not a freedom from anything, but a freedom in and of Grace.

But if we forget for a moment that all this is here where we are now, we will be looking for it in the future and we will lose it. Let us never be tempted to believe for a moment that we will receive God's grace tomorrow. Let us never believe that our student or patient will receive God's grace after we give a treatment, pray, or meditate. No, our wisdom consists in knowing that those who turn to us are already under God's grace—not that our prayer is going to establish God's grace.

Our prayer is the acknowledgment of the omnipresence of God's grace, so that the Grace, surrounding our student or patient before the world began, now comes into visible manifestation because of our knowing this truth, because of our prayer, meditation, or treatment.

We of ourselves would be nothing but for the grace of God. It is by the grace of God that we have the awareness of Omnipresence, Omnipotence, and Omniscience, that we have access to the wisdom of the world, the wisdom of all time and space.

Dwell in Christ. Be that man who has his being in Christ, living by Grace. Walk this earth for one purpose only: to show forth God's glory.

· 10 ·

"Choose You"

ONLY THAT FUNCTIONS IN YOUR LIFE which functions as an activity of your consciousness. In your humanhood, before you come to know the truth, what is operating in your consciousness is a combination of things: beliefs, theories, inhibitions, ignorance, prenatal influences, and the superstitions of your parents, grandparents, and great-grandparents. They have been impressed upon your consciousness from the time of your birth and operate in your consciousness to make your life whatever it is. If you were born or have come into a very good and harmonious life or if your experience is discordant, unpleasant, or evil, you are the beneficiary or the victim of these influences. You, yourself, have not been master of your life; you, yourself, have had no control over your life.

There is nothing you can do about the past except forget it. There is a great deal, however, that you can do about the present and the future. You have the power of determining the rightness and harmony of your life or of putting up with its discords and inharmonies; you have the right to make a choice whether you will let prenatal influences, early environmental and personal experiences dominate your life or whether you will now change and begin to know the truth, and let the truth make you free. "Choose you this day whom ye will serve," [1] God or mammon. This is not merely a quotation: this is a command, and it requires action.

"Ye cannot serve God and mammon." [2] You are commanded to make a choice. What choice? Whether you will serve God or mammon. But how can you choose unless you know the difference between serving God and serving mammon? Will you serve "this world" or "My kingdom [which] is not of this world"?[3] Will you live in "this world" or "My kingdom"? It does not mean leaving one place for another place; it does not mean dying in order to go to heaven.

The Master prayed "not that thou shouldest take them out of the world, but that thou shouldest keep them from the evil. They are not of the world, even as I am not of the world." [4] To choose, then, does not mean to go to some ashrama, mountaintop, or waterfront resort and desert your family or the world. It does not mean that at all. It means to remain in this world but not to let yourself be touched by its temptations, its iniquities, or its limitations.

To What Degree Will You Devote Yourself to Attaining Christhood?

When you come to a message of this nature, you must understand that whatever you take into your consciousness is going to be the determining factor in your life. You alone determine to what degree you will attain Christhood. If you wish to devote an hour to truth on Sunday, it will certainly benefit you in some measure. If you decide to devote an hour to truth every day, it will benefit you that much more. If you decide that during some part of every hour of every day you will allow some truth to circulate in your consciousness, there will be that much more of fruitage in your life.

A consciousness imbued with truth becomes a law of harmony, not only to you but to those who come in contact with you. You cannot be the light of the world and keep that light hidden under a bushel basket. If you are the light of the world, the world beholds that light and benefits by it. But you cannot be the light except in proportion as truth is consciously embodied in your consciousness.

This world is a world of getting, achieving, accomplishing, struggling, striving. It is a world of two powers. To some extent, however, you have already left that world if you have come to realize that life need not be lived by power, by might, or by struggle, but that life can be lived by Grace and that you are on the path to experience that Grace in the greatest possible measure. If you have any other goal than to know God and to seek the realization of the kingdom of God and His righteousness, however, you are setting up a barrier between yourself and your ultimate harmony.

Nothing in the lives, the teachings, or the revelations of the mystics of the world would authorize anyone to use God as his servant to do something for him. But many mystical teachings indicate that we are servants of God, children of God, under the dominion and grace of God, that we are the instruments through which God appears.

Choose Whether You Will Make God a Servant
or Whether You Will Surrender to God's Will

Choose whether you want God to do your will and supply you with what you think you need, or whether you wish to enter a spiritual realm of life in which you surrender your will to God.

Not my will, but "thy will be done" [5] *in me. Thy grace is my sufficiency—not what I tell You I need or want. I surrender my needs and my wants and accept Thy grace. Father, the All-knowing within me, feed me in accordance with Thy grace and Thy wishes.*

Accept and realize the nature of God as Omniscience, the All-knowing. Ask for nothing; seek nothing; abide within yourself in an expectancy of God's grace, God's love, peace, abundance, and companionship. When you have that Companionship, It appears outwardly as the right human companionship. When you have the abundance of God, It appears outwardly in an infinite form that will bless you without cursing you. Your mind does not have to work because you are turning within only for the purpose of receptivity, of receiving the benediction of God's grace.

"Choose you this day" whether you are going to be in this world and think of yourself as a human being going to God for your daily needs or whether you are going to accept yourself as the child of God who is heir to all the heavenly riches. Choose, right now, and if you choose to be the child of God, never pray to God for anything except that His Spirit be upon you, that His grace be realized within you—not that God do something for you, but that you awaken to His presence.

As you take this attitude, you will hear the Master within say to you, " 'My peace give I unto you: not as the world giveth,' [6] not as you think you may need or want it, but *My* peace, divine peace, the peace that is wisdom and love, the peace that will not deceive you and will not be lacking in quantity or quality."

CHOOSE BETWEEN SERVING GOOD AND EVIL
OR SERVING OMNIPOTENCE

You are called upon to choose whether you will accept two powers or rest in Omnipotence. Since God is omnipotent, there is no other power, and so evil is not a power in the presence of God. Sin, disease, depression, unemployment, and lack—these are not powers in the presence of God. Because God is omnipotent, the all-power, you never seek the power of God for anything under any consideration. You do not need it. Having Omnipotence, there is no other power.

You do not make a blanket statement, however, that evil, sin, disease, and lack are not power. You recognize that *in the presence of God realized*, evil is not power; *in the presence of God realized*, error cannot exist, whether it is a condition of weather, a condition of food, a condition of poison, or a condition of bullets or bombs. *In the presence of the Almighty*, there are no other powers. There cannot be an Almighty and other powers, too, and this Almighty is everywhere present. Right where you are on the highway, in adultery, in disease, or on the cross, God is there in the midst of you.

God already is omnipresent, the all-presence; God already is omnipotent, the all-power; God already is omniscient, the all-knowing. Therefore do not go to God for anything. Go within yourself and awaken—awaken to the realization that God already is. All that the Father has is awaiting your awakening, your acceptance, your realization.

CHOOSE TO ACCEPT OMNIPRESENCE AS
THE ONLY PRESENCE

When you are untaught of the Spirit, you are likely to look at your empty pocketbook, your sick body or sinful mind, and declare your barrenness. But in that moment of barrenness, if you would realize that the law of love, of life, and of God is operating in you now as Omnipotence, Omnipresence, and Omniscience, you would take the attitude of being a beholder, and in days, weeks, or a few months, the sin and the disease would leave your body, and the barrenness would leave your mind.

The kingdom of God is within me, the allness of God. God is the creative principle of my being, the maintaining and sustaining principle. God is the very life of me; therefore, I am immortal; and neither life nor death can separate me from the care of God. I am under the jurisdiction of God. Whether on this plane of life, a future plane of life, or some previous plane of life, always I am inseparable and indivisible from God.

If you consciously embody that in your life, you manifest it in your daily experience. If you do not consciously embody it in your life, the truth cannot set you free. Are you in bondage to any form of lack or limitation? Are you in bondage to unhappiness? Are you in bondage to ill health, to old age? Then you are in bondage to it because you are not consciously knowing the truth. You are not consciously embodying within yourself the acknowledgment of God's presence within you, God's power within you, the omnipotence of God functioning as you, the omniscience and the omnipresence of God where you are.

God does not move away from you in your sins or in your lack, but the acknowledgment of God within you will eliminate the sins because where the consciousness of God is, sin cannot dwell; where the consciousness of God is, lack cannot exist. Acknowledge the presence of God in your soul, in your mind, in your body. Acknowledge the presence of God in your business. Acknowledge the presence of God in whatever your work may be. Always acknowledge God as the Source.

Choose To Claim No Qualities As Your Own

When the Master said, "Why callest thou me good? there is none good but one, that is, God," [7] he revealed clearly that if there is any good quality about any one of us, it is the God-quality shining through. Of yourself, you are not good, and whatever goodness there is, is but God's grace flowing through you. Whatever goodness, benevolence, or virtue is evident in your life, whatever intelligence or capacity for spiritual thought is the grace of God expressing through and as you.

But just as you should not claim to be good, so go a step further and do not claim any evil in yourself. "For that which I do I allow not: for what I would, that do I not; but what I hate, that do I. . . . Now then it is no more I that do it, but sin that dwelleth in me." [8] Paul recognized the potentiality for evil in him as the carnal mind, not himself. Always it is the carnal mind that is the tempter, tempting you to believe that God is separate and apart from you.

So whether evil comes in the form of a sinful desire or in the form of sickness, learn to recognize it as a temptation, not as a part of you, but as something that is tempting you to believe in a selfhood or a power apart from God. Do not identify evil with yourself, but remember not to identify good with yourself either.

102

Identify all good as of God; identify yourself as the transparency through which the qualities and the quantities of the Father are appearing. Nothing is outside of the possible as long as you are not claiming any qualities, virtues, or quantities as your own, but are acknowledging that you are the instrument through which the grace of God is acting.

This is choosing. Choose not to be an inlet or an outlet for the carnal mind which Paul tells us "is not subject to the law of God, neither indeed can be," [9] not to be "the natural man [who] receiveth not the things of the Spirit of God." [10] Choose not to be this man of earth but to be the son of God.

CHOOSE TO CARRY A BENEDICTION
WHEREVER YOU GO

As you look out on those around you, walk in the remembrance of your sonship and let the grace of God which has made you the son bless whomever you meet. Carry in your consciousness a peace-be-still to the errors of this world. As you sit in your home, realize the peace of God that is upon you and upon those who are a part of your consciousness. As you go into a hotel to register or into a restaurant or an airplane, remember that the peace of God that blesses you blesses the place whereon you stand. Wherever you go, carry the peace of God with you because the peace of God was not given to you for you. Instead, you begin to realize, "This is God's peace and God's grace that I am to bestow."

What did Jesus Christ do with the grace of God that was upon him? Did he go off to the seaside or to a mountain to live with it for himself or did he walk up and down the land bestowing that peace upon all the troubled souls who came to him? What did Gautama the Buddha do after he sat under the bodhi-tree and received the Spirit of God? He immediately walked up and down the whole length of India establishing ashramas, places where people could go to be healed and blessed. What did Moses do after he had his mountaintop experience of having God speak to him and reveal the Name? He took the Hebrews out of slavery and at the risk of his life led them into their freedom. What did Elijah do with the grace of God that was given him? Even when he was being persecuted, he stood by waiting for the "seven thousand . . . all the knees which have not bowed unto Baal," [11] so that he could return to them and give out to them the grace of God which he had received. The grace of God fed, sustained, and supported him, just as It fed and supported Jesus Christ in his ministry.

Everyone who has ever received the Spirit of God has been ordained to pass It on in some way or other to all those receptive and responsive to It in their community and world. Forty-eight hours after I received my first spiritual experience, I was doing healing work. It was not meant that I should receive the grace of God and have the experience of ordination just so that I might be healthy, wealthy, and wise for the rest of my days, but that I might be an instrument for the Spirit.

The apple trees, the peach trees, and the pear trees do not use up their own fruit. They are fed and sustained by the divine Life, but the fruitage they bear is meant for the world. So it is that those who are a part of a spiritual ministry are fed and sustained, but it probably takes only a grain of the Spirit to maintain them, and the rest has to be poured out to all those who are receptive.

A spiritual ministry is not only a sacred one but it is a secret one. You do not voice the fact that you have come to the realization that you are a child of God and an heir to all the heavenly blessings. You maintain that awareness in your own consciousness sacredly and secretly, and you do not bless people by outwardly or openly speaking truth to them, but by silently letting the peace of God flow through you to them.

You really have nothing to give the world until the Spirit of God is upon you and you are ordained. Then you will not have to go out seeking to shed your light. The world that is in darkness will come to you for light, but only because you have chosen to serve the Spirit of God within every person.

· II ·

Spiritual Supply

I<small>N THE METAPHYSICAL WORLD</small>, it is common practice to try to demonstrate supply, companionship, home, or transportation. In a mystical message such as The Infinite Way, however, this is an incorrect basis from which to work because a person is then working from the premise of I-have-not. That is virtually sin; it is acknowledging a sense of separation from God, from good, from completeness and infinity. We do not go outside our consciousness to demonstrate anything because the infinite divine Consciousness is our individual consciousness and embodies infinity. Therefore, we have nothing to do with drawing supply to us, but rather with drawing the indwelling supply forth from us.

As long as we are living in a material sense of world, we will think of supply as purely material, which always consists of something external to us to be acquired: money, a home, automobiles. But in the real world of Spirit, supply is not external to us, nor is it ever to be acquired, attained, or sought after, because in the spiritual realm supply is what *I* am: *I* am the bread; *I* am the meat; *I* am the water. With no thought whatsoever of anyone or anything in the external realm, we turn within and commune with our inner being and abide in the realization of a completeness inherent in our Self.

When we understand that, we can look at everyone and see how wholly independent each one is of the other because of the principle of Self-completeness. The one Life is caring for us and drawing unto us all that is necessary for our fulfillment. This Self-completeness which we are and which supplies us so abundantly is not really for us: it is poured into and through us as fruitage to be shared.

Before we can begin to share, however, we must rise out of the material sense of life that thinks it must get. We do not have to acquire, strive, or struggle: we only have to stand still in the realization of Self-completeness and Self-containment.

The Universal Nature of Supply

"I and my Father are one." [1] In my realization of this relationship, I let the Infinite Invisible draw unto me from the skies, the clouds, the air, the earth, and from every part of the universe—from all six continents and many islands—all that is necessary for my particular unfoldment.

But this is not merely your supply or my supply, because that, too, is limitation. Just inserting the word "your" or "my" brings about a limitation. The word "my" is used in the beginning stages, but later, as consciousness unfolds, we realize that because of the universal nature of truth, Self-completeness is the truth about all men.

In speaking of the sun or the moon we would never say "my" sun or moon, or "your" sun or moon. We speak of the sun as universal light and warmth to both the saint and the sinner, the

107

white and the black, the Oriental and the Occidental, the Jew and the Gentile. Ultimately we begin to look at the subject of supply in the same light and never refer to my supply or yours, because when I think of supply as personal, I am so "finitizing" it that I am turning it into a material concept instead of truth. If I want to speak truthfully about supply, I must release any and all personal sense of ownership; I must lose all sense of limitation by not claiming anything as mine.

"The earth is the Lord's, and the fulness thereof.[2] . . . Son, thou art ever with me, and all that I have is thine." [3] I must not be so egotistical as to think of that as being addressed to Joel alone. I must understand that it is being addressed to the sons of God. If I personalize it in any way and believe that God is speaking only to me, what have I done to you? And if I shut out one of you, even the greatest sinner, I have shut myself out, for there is only one infinite divine Self, and that one Self is Self-contained, Self-maintained, and Self-sustained. The material sense of supply personalizes supply. When you think of your supply or mine, it is always limited, but when you think of all supply as the Father's, it is infinite.

Why then are so many persons limited? There is only one answer. The world entertains a material sense of supply, and as long as it does, there will be limitation. In reality there is no such thing as lack or even abundance. There is only each person's individual experience of abundance or lack.

Opening the Doors of Supply

Supply is spiritual; therefore, supply is infinite. If you were to open yourself to accept God's grace, then all the necessary supply would be added to you. Even those who have not been taught spiritual living can experience abundance by opening their consciousness to some measure of human love and coming out of the shell of self in which they live: by giving, sharing, serving, and by a little more friendliness. Never doubt but that those who are not receiving supply are in some way barring it from themselves. What they are doing differs with each person.

There are some persons who talk about their pride, which is a lot of utter nonsense. There are others who have never known a real feeling of gratitude, love, giving, or of sharing. I do not mean giving to their children or to their families: I mean giving and sharing impersonally. They are shutting out supply because while it may be right outside the door, it cannot roll up to anyone's door except as he opens his consciousness. In one way or another, those who lack, lack because they themselves have shut the door to infinite abundance. It is not done in any premeditated fashion: it is always done ignorantly.

Many experiences have come to my attention of persons who came to the realization that they were shutting out supply by not giving or sharing, and who then decided to tithe, thereby changing the whole nature of their demonstration, even when it was not on the highest level of spiritual realization but at the level of helping or sharing with the neighbor. There is not merely one way in which to experience abundance: there is provision at every level of consciousness. But the highest demonstration is the demonstration of the consciousness of the presence of God. It is this that fulfills all your needs.

At the mystical level of consciousness, thought must never be permitted to dwell on supply as if it were something to be attained or even earned or deserved. Supply is the realization of *I* in the midst of us that has come that we might have life and that we might have it more abundantly.

Do you begin to see the difference between these two worlds: the outer world by which we seem to be living on the things that are without and the inner world in which we realize that even those things that seem to come to us from without are really being drawn to us by the Spirit that is within us? We abide in the truth that the invisible Life of us is that which draws from the external world what is needed in our individual experience.

RELEASING IMPERSONAL LOVE

Regardless of what area of life we may be considering, we must never forget the great principle of impersonalization. Has not every bit of trouble in which we have been involved come either from personalizing God or personalizing error? Now we must take another step and impersonalize supply so there is no such thing as my supply or yours: there is Self-containment, Self-completeness, Self-fulfillment.

In the awareness of our relationship of oneness are found completeness and allness. This oneness with the Father is my fullness and completeness, but not mine separate from yours. You have the same fullness, the same completeness, the same perfection. You need only awaken to it, and we awaken to that realization in the degree that we can impersonalize God, impersonalize error, impersonalize supply, and impersonalize love.

The only way in which we can impersonalize love and express divine love is by knowing that we do not have the power to give or to withhold. We can merely be the instruments through which it takes place. In spite of all we know, however, humanly we will be tempted to love or to withhold love on a personal basis, to give more here and less there. All this is a barrier to the demonstration of real harmony in our lives. Each one of us has to have a period during the day in which we let ourselves become the transparency for the Spirit to bless our home, business, or our nation, and with no personal sense of these.

Humanly we may have a greater affection for one than for others. That has to be because the others are responsible for it. Actually, I could not possibly give more human affection to those who are not giving it or sharing it because they are not calling it forth. Those who call forth affection in the greatest degree receive the greatest measure of it. That, I admit, is true from the human standpoint.

But that does not prevent me at least once a day from going into my inner stillness and realizing that I am neither giving to nor withholding love from anyone. I am now the transparency through which the grace of God embraces all persons everywhere. Then their receptivity will make for them a full life, or their lack of receptivity will let it squander itself out here. I am responsible only for letting the light shine. I am not responsible for making somebody open his door to receive it. That is his function.

Our greatest gift to this world is not our personal service to our family. Our greatest value is the measure in which we can sit still and be such a clear transparency that God's love can flow into our household, business, and nation. This is impersonalizing love, and it is that impersonal love that meets the need individually and collectively.

On some levels of human life, a person should humanly be very loving, charitable, and benevolent, because that is his only access to peace and harmony. As he gives, so does he receive. As he sows, so does he reap—but not at the spiritual level. At that level, the highest spiritual experience is divine love, and this is not a love that you or I can give or withhold. This is something that flows through us, and it works itself out on the human level.

Supply is infinite, but there must be receptivity. Everyone will say, "Oh, I'll receive all the supply you'll give me." It does not work that way. We can have all the supply we will give. But that is where the barrier is—the unwillingness to give. That is where the lack or limitation is.

Are the starving people of the world to blame for their lack of food? No, not any more than we were to blame when we were ignorant of this truth, or than we are to blame because we are not enjoying greater harmony. Those who are suffering from lack are shutting out supply through ignorance. Some of them have allowed their nature to become unloving, and where there is no love there is no abundance. They have allowed themselves to become ingrown, separate and apart from their fellow men. They have developed a consciousness of "get" instead of "give," even of getting something for nothing. This ignorance, however, is not their fault. They are just hypnotized, and this hypnotism will continue until there is an awakening within them that drives them to something higher than material sense and breaks through that universal hypnotism.

Make a practice once a day of sitting quietly and giving no human love to anyone, but, on the other hand, having no negative emotions: no hate, envy, jealousy, malice, revenge, or indifference. Do not have these, and do not have any desire to love anybody. Sit quietly for a moment and let the Spirit of God, divine love, flow through your consciousness to your household, to your family, to the neighbors, to the city, the state, the community, the nation, and finally the world.

Thy grace is the sufficiency of this world. Let Thy grace be upon the world and be realized in all human consciousness. Let Thy grace be established on earth as it is in heaven.

112

Then be silent for a few moments while the Spirit flows. You have given no love; you have withheld no love; you have not been unloving: you have merely been still, and you have let the still, small Voice be heard throughout all human consciousness.

· 12 ·

The Power and Dominion

THERE ARE TWO WORLDS: there is the world of the man of earth, who is not under the law of God; and then there is the world of the son of God, the world of the spiritual universe in which life is lived not by taking thought, but by divine Grace. While we already know about this outer world, we do not yet know enough about the life by Grace.

God gave us dominion over everything there is between the skies and the bottom of the sea. But bit by bit, we have surrendered our dominion and become prodigal sons. We have turned our back on the kingdom of God and lived in a material sense of world made up of human beings, groveling at the feet of some unknown God, praying for crumbs, when all the time the true God in the midst of us made us heirs of the entire kingdom.

In the recognition of our divine sonship, we must once again accept our dominion, and this means that we create our own world. The world does not create conditions for us; people do not create conditions for us. We are not the victims of politics, of war or dictators, of circumstances or conditions; we are not the victims of sin or disease: we are the victims of what we, ourselves, have created. Never again must we give dominion to man or circumstances, but henceforth, we must live under the laws revealed to us by the Master Christian.

LIFE MORE ABUNDANT

"I am come that they might have life, and that they might have it more abundantly." [1] The word *"I"* used in that statement does not mean Jesus. It does not mean your teacher or practitioner. This *I* is your very Self, the saviour and redeemer at the center of your being, and therefore, you dare not go to God even for supply because you already have *I*, the Spirit of God, in the midst of you.

"I am the resurrection." [2] This truth would be of no avail to you if it applied only to Jesus. The truth is that the power of resurrection—the resurrection of your body, of your health, your wealth, your marriage, your home, or your family—is within you. But you will never demonstrate this as long as you are expecting it to come from some source outside of you—even if it is a holy person—for *I* in the midst of you am come that you might have life.

To yourself, this moment, say the word *"I,"* softly, gently: *I, I.* That very *I* in the midst of you is the law of resurrection. That very Selfhood, that very spiritual presence of God is working in you to resurrect your body, your health, your family, your love, your career. If you accept the testimony of the world, by the time you are forty-five, you will not be able to find employment because the world will claim that you are too old, and by the time you are sixty or sixty-five, you will be retired to await the coming of death. Accepting that, you permit it to be a law unto you, and then you become the victim of the suggestions of this world.

If, however, you understand that *I* in the midst of you is God, then you will know that that *I* is the presence of God that has come that you might have the life more abundant, not life until forty, fifty, sixty, or seventy, but life eternal. *I* am come even to restore the years that have sped by in ignorance of the truth that God is in the midst of you. That *I* now becomes a law of resurrection unto your entire experience.

It takes spiritual discernment to recognize that *I* in the midst of you is God, that Its function there is to be your bread, meat, wine, and water, and that nobody has to go out to get anything for you because you already have meat the world knows not of. Every time you are faced with an appearance of barrenness— emptiness, lack, or limitation—hug this truth to yourself sacredly and secretly:

Thank You, Father, I have a divine substance the world knows not of. Neither life nor death can separate me from the love of God —neither life nor death. The place whereon I stand is holy ground, whether on this side of the veil or the other side, in sickness or in health, in purity or in sin. "I can do all things through Christ which strengtheneth me." [3]

The Christ is one name for the son of God. The other name is *I.* They both mean the same thing: the presence, the power, the wisdom, and the love of God. The Christ that is your saviour, resurrection, and mediator is the presence of God that was established in you in the beginning and which you have been seeking in the outer world.

People are seeking God, turning from one religion to another, from one teaching to another, one teacher to another, until finally they discover one who will say to them, "But you have It within you. That which you are seeking, you already embody within yourself. It constitutes your very being." Then they will understand why they can live a life of absolute freedom in Christ.

116

BE A BENEDICTION

As you go about your daily living, breathe silently, sacredly, secretly: " 'My peace I give unto you: not as the world giveth.' [4] *My* peace, the Christ-peace, give I unto thee. 'Let not your heart be troubled,' [5] neither let it be afraid." Your function is to be a benediction so that wherever you travel you can bestow God's grace on those still in darkness.

Probably the most difficult part of this practice is that you have to begin inside your own home. Since you know everybody there so well, it is hard for you to see that the members of your own household are all saints—but they are. And if you are seeing them as other than saints, you are the one who is in error, not they, because God never made any other than a saint.

I know as well as everybody else that family living is not the easiest thing in the world. It is such a close relationship, and we are so apt to show the worst side of ourselves to those closest to us, that from a human standpoint this is very difficult. But it is not difficult from a spiritual standpoint. Something will take place if you are willing to sit down for five minutes each day to realize the truth:

This is the household of God—not my household. All those who dwell herein are offspring of God, joint-heirs of God, fellow-saints, not dependent upon each other, but sharing with each other God's grace. God's grace governs, maintains, and sustains all who are within this household.

The father in the home has qualities of thought to share with the mother and the children. The mother has qualities of love and companionship to share with the father and the children. The children have qualities of God to share with the parents. But none

117

of them is dependent on the others. They mutually share those qualities that God has given them.

Hold no member of the family in bondage to his sins, to his errors, or to his disposition. Realize that whatever is not of God must disappear because it has no law of God to sustain it. Recognize that *I* in the midst of each member of this household is God, and it will not take too long before you will find a greater degree of harmony in the household.

You can begin to practice the same truth for your neighbors, relatives, and friends, for your community, business, school, and profession, and before many years go by, you will be doing world work. You will be embracing all the trouble spots of the world in your consciousness, realizing that if you feel there is any evil in them, it is really in your perception of them. There can be no evil in them. God did not create one nation good and another bad, one person well and another sick. Therefore, you have dominion— dominion over your concepts.

If you accept sinning people into your consciousness, you will have sin. If you accept sick people into your consciousness, you will have sickness. If you accept evil people, you will have evil. But if you remember what the Master said, "I stand at the door, and knock," [6] do you know what would happen? Do you know what happens when you open your consciousness and say, "Enter"? You have made way for the Spirit of God to flow forth into your experience.

SATISFY THE INNER LONGING
TO HAVE SPIRITUAL IDENTITY RECOGNIZED

When you are thinking of a member of your family or of some of the politicians—and I use that word in its worst sense—or when

118

you think of the so-called dictators of the world, just remember that that *I* in the midst of them is knocking at the door of your consciousness for entrance. Do not open your consciousness to their humanhood because you are opening your consciousness to an illusory picture. Rather open your consciousness to the *I* of every individual.

Do not think of the members of your family in their humanhood. We all know what they are in their humanhood. We may not like all of them, but turn from that and remember that the *I* of them is standing at the door of your consciousness seeking admittance, and you will heal all who are receptive and responsive.

Your dominion in your home or any other place consists in the truth that what is called "this world"[7] exists only in your thought. Out here, sin, disease, death, lack, and limitation do not exist. If you are experiencing them, you are experiencing them in your own thought and projecting the image outwardly. It is like a moving picture. The picture is actually on the film, but it is projected onto the screen, and, if you did not know better, you would think the picture is on the screen, when it really is on the film. In our ignorance we think that there are sick and sinning people out here. No, they are in our own thought. That is the only place they exist —no other place. The proof of that is that when someone turns to an enlightened consciousness, one that does not accept sin or disease, the image or picture dissolves and disappears.

You may say that you are sick, in sin, or in poverty. But I cannot accept that because I have already accepted the Bible which says that God made all that was made and all that God made is good and anything that God did not make was not made. Therefore, there can be no such thing as evil, sin, disease, or death. In my consciousness I accept you as the Christ. Who can convince me

119

that you are sick, in sin, or dying? Nobody! As long as I can hold onto the truth, " 'Thou art the Christ, the Son of the living God[8] . . . Neither do I condemn thee,'[9] neither do I find any fault in thee," you must eventually respond. Since I have not accepted your mortality in my thought, it must die.

The *I* of me is knocking at the door of your consciousness wanting you to say, "I know thee who thou art. 'Thou art the Christ, the Son of the living God.' " The *I* of you is knocking at the door of my consciousness and begging me to see you as you are, not as you humanly appear to be. You want me to behold you as the image of God, the way you were created in the beginning before time began. None of you wants me to see you as you are humanly.

You come to be recognized in your spiritual identity so that whatever is mortal of you may be dissolved. You may have thought it was so that you might be healed, reformed, employed, or blessed. That is the decoy, but the truth is that you come to be recognized in your spiritual identity. That is why I am in this work. It is not to heal, reform, or enrich anybody. It is to behold and reveal to you the Christ of your own identity. As I give recognition to It, in some measure I bring It forth into expression.

In the morning, there is usually time for five or ten minutes of quiet, and if you do not have the time, make the time. Let something else wait, and then take those who are nearest and closest to you in your household, and begin to look through the appearance and recognize that right there in the midst of them the son of God dwells. As you bear witness to that Christ of God in them, you will see how very soon they will begin to respond and show forth more of their Christhood and less of their mortality.

So it continues until eventually we are not as aware of human beings as we once were, not quite so aware of how they look or what they are wearing. There is an inner discernment of Something that is shining through their eyes, sometimes even in those who themselves do not know that It is there.

BEARING WITNESS TO THE CHRIST-IDENTITY

Always remember that there is an *I*, standing at the door of your consciousness begging your acknowledgment and recognition. Many times a day, you must close your eyes for a second and say, "Yes, I recognize my Christhood, the *I* in the midst of me." But then as someone enters your household, or even your thought, remember that the *I* of him is also knocking at the door of your consciousness asking to be admitted.

Do you know why a person who is not living up to the full integrity of his humanhood does not like to be condemned? He knows truly that it is not he who is bad. It is something that temporarily has dominion over him. In the same way, very few persons really like to be praised for their goodness, their benevolence, or their virtue. They would rather say, "No, no, no." They know that that is not a quality of themselves. It is something that is shining through them. We do not want to be praised, but we do not object to having the Christ of us praised and acknowledged. We do not want to be condemned because the evil that we do, we do not want to do: it is something that is impinging upon us from the outside world.

The major factor in leaving the two worlds for the one world is acknowledging the *I*. The *I* of me wants me to acknowledge my Christhood. It wants me to settle down and be still and know that *I* within is God. Every person who ever comes to me is unknowingly begging and pleading that I recognize his true identity, the *I* of him.

121

You cannot possibly bear witness to the Christ-identity of your parents, your husband, your wife, or your children without its eventually softening and mellowing them. You may be assured that the *I* of every member of your family is begging you to see him as he is, not as he appears to be while he is under the influence of this world.

The sad part is that most persons keep right on seeing those around them as they *appear* to be and pin the very errors on to them that they dislike; whereas if only they could see the word *"I"* over the heads of each one of them and realize that the *I* of them is knocking at the door of their consciousness for recognition, they would be lifting them out of these errors. But do not do this openly and outwardly. Enter into the silent sanctuary of your own being and there give recognition to the *I* of everyone you meet. Watch for that *I* over his head, and you will see It there. It is there; everyone has It; and, oh, how It is begging for recognition.

Conducting a Successful Spiritual Healing Ministry

If we insist on seeing each other as the man of earth, as mortal man—some good, some bad, some well, some sick—then that is the world we are creating for ourselves. But if we have been granted any degree of spiritual discernment so that we can behold the *I* of every individual and receive It into our consciousness, acknowledge It, welcome It, and bless It, then we transform our world.

From then on, we will not have sick people coming into our consciousness. It will be like a well-known practitioner who was a close friend of mine and who was visited by another practitioner who had heard about the great healing work this man was doing. The practitioner found him in an office answering the telephone —two lines going constantly—and always he was saying, "Yes, I will take care of it." "Yes, just leave it with me." "Yes, I'll take care of it right away. Yes." And that went on and on and on.

The man waited for about an hour and could not get in, and then finally came to me and complained, "This is terrible. All these people are calling for help, and he promises to give it, but he never once gave any one of them a treatment."

My response was, "You don't understand. This man has a different kind of practice from yours. You see, he doesn't have any sick people coming to him."

How could any one of us have a successful healing practice, if it were a spiritual practice, if we accepted sick people into our consciousness? Are we taught how to heal disease? Do we know anything about anatomy, physiology, biology, germs, or broken bones? Of course not! The only reason we can bring forth a healing is that the only ones who come to us are the sons of God. The healing consists in recognizing that.

Everyone who enters my consciousness has a sign over his head saying "I," and that I is knocking at the door of my consciousness, begging me to recognize It, and when I do this, his mortality evaporates, and something takes place to bring harmony into his experience. But it does not come through having sick people coming to me for healing, or sinning people to be reformed. It comes through one principle: through spiritual discernment. I see the I. I recognize It, I accept It, I welcome It, bless It, and sooner or later the person who asked for help has recognized the I of his own identity.

ONE WORLD

Do you see that there are two worlds: the world of "My kingdom" and the world in which you look out and see male and female, young and old, sick and well, the world in which you sit in judgment on the appearances of the world? But you must always bear in mind that there are not really two worlds: there is only one, the world that God created. There really is no such thing as an unreal world or counterfeit world. There is only one world, and this world is that world.

We entertain a false concept about this magnificent world, so that we become aware of hatred, bias, bigotry, envy, jealousy, malice, disease, sin, fear, and man's inhumanity to man. Because we are judging by appearances, because we are seeing through finite sense, we say, "What a terrible world!" And yet there is no such world because God created all that was created, and all that God created is good.

Every mystic who has attained the mystical consciousness has known and revealed that God is Spirit and that this is a spiritual universe. What the Master called "this world" is the world of material sense, but the world could not accept that interpretation. Today, however, the idea that there is no physical body and no physical universe but that what is called matter is mind is being more widely accepted.

We are in the golden age where science and religion must come together in the realization that the real world is a world of Spirit, of Consciousness, and that Consciousness is really the principle of life. This universe is a projection of Consciousness, and your world and mine are of the nature of our state of consciousness. Our world is the product of the measure of the *I* that we are showing forth. If we were wholly unconditioned, then our world would be wholly and entirely spiritual, incorporeal, harmonious, eternal, and immortal. But we have been able to manifest only a certain degree or measure of that infinite divine Consciousness, and, therefore, our world is exactly the measure of divine Consciousness that we can realize. Whatever still remains of error in our life represents the degree of our darkness, our unillumined or conditioned state.

Moreover, because of human birth and conditioning, we are fettered by the sense of physicality. From the moment of conception, a physical sense of body has been built up in us. But *I* is not physical. *I* has never entered a cell any more than *I* has entered a physical body. After thirty-five years of active healing work, I can tell you that the only barrier to better healing work is that very limitation or conditioning which still operates in our consciousness to make us believe that our patient has a physical body that has to have its fever reduced, its lump removed, or a condition changed. Consciously, we know better. We know that we are *I;* our patient is *I*, incorporeal, spiritual, harmonious, and whole. And yet there are times when we are asked for help that that old, old conditioning comes to the fore and says, "What can I do about it?" or, "I'd better sit up all night." Why? Because we still find occasions for having to rise out of the belief that we are physical and have physical bodies.

Dominion comes through recognizing the spiritual nature and identity of every individual. This transforms our world and gives us dominion over sin, sickness, and ultimately over death. In the recognition of our spiritual identity we are now tabernacling with that which was never born and will never die. Jesus could say, "Before Abraham was, I am," [10] because he knew that *I* was never born, not even immaculately. *I* never was born, and *I* never will die. Even if you crucify and bury the body, *I* still will never die. *I* will be with you until the end of the world, and that *I* is always crying out for recognition.

Is there any power that can limit I*? Is there any power in heaven or on earth greater than* I AM*? I* am the only power there is, and besides Me, there is no power.

Ponder that; contemplate that; meditate upon that. Face the waves with that, the storms, the depressions, the epidemics, and the threats of war. Face all these with the realization that there are no evil men; there are no evil powers. All there is, is a physical finite *sense* of God, man, and the universe.

God has been reduced to statues, and God's power to medals. God and God's power have been reduced to men and names. But *I* is not person: *I* is God, and besides that *I* there is no power in heaven or on earth, for *I* alone am.

In the presence of this spiritual realization, the material sense of existence loses its claim to power, just as you have witnessed that with spiritual realization even physical symptoms have disappeared: growths have dissolved; fevers have been dissipated. In other words, physical sense dissolves in the presence of the realization of *I* as God.

"Be still, and know that I am God." [11] Be still, and then you will see how this divine impulse comes through. Be still and let the *I*, which is Omniscience, Omnipotence, and Omnipresence and needs no help from anyone, come through, and watch harmony established on earth as it is in heaven, and the one world of heaven and earth revealed.

List Of Scriptural References

1. *Opening the Door to Infinity*

1. Isaiah 2:22.
2. Revelation 3:20.
3. John 14:27.
4. Luke 16:31.
5. Luke 4:18.
6. Matthew 13:46.
7. John 10:30.
8. Philippians 2:5.
9. Galatians 2:20.
10. II Corinthians 5:4.
11. Matthew 23:9.
12. Genesis 18:28–32.
13. Matthew 26:52.
14. John 18:36.

2. *The Nature of Spiritual Attainment*

1. Matthew 7:14.
2. John 18:36.
3. Ephesians 5:14.
4. John 5:8.

3. *Easter, a Rising Out of Material Sense*

1. Luke 15:31.
2. John 10:30.
3. Matthew 4:4.
4. John 14:27.

4. *The Operation of the "Arm of Flesh" and the Operation of Truth*

1. John 14:10.
2. Philippians 4:13.
3. Psalm 91:10.
4. Psalm 91:1.
5. John 10:30.
6. John 19:11.
7. Isaiah 26:3.

5. *The World of Material Sense and the World of Spiritual Discernment*

1. John 18:36.
2. Luke 15:31.
3. Isaiah 45:2.
4. Matthew 3:17.

6. *Making the Transition from Personal Sense to Spiritual Being*

1. I Corinthians 2:14.
2. Matthew 4:4.
3. John 8:58.
4. John 15:13.
5. Psalm 24:1.
6. Luke 15:31.

7. Isaiah 2:22.   9. Luke 23:34.
8. Psalm 46:10.

7. The Consciousness of Omnipresence

1. Psalm 23:4.   5. Matthew 28:20.
2. Genesis 18:32.   6. John 10:10.
3. Luke 22:42.   7. John 14:6.
4. Hebrews 13:5.

8. The Way to Fulfillment: Right Identification

1. Ezekiel 21:27.   4. Luke 3:7.
2. Matthew 19:17.   5. Joel 25:5.
3. Matthew 21:12.   6. Psalm 16:11

9. Becoming Instruments of Grace Through Reconciliation

1. I John 4:20.   4. Romans 8:17.
2. Matthew 25:40.   5. Matthew 4:19.
3. John 18:36.

10. "Choose You"

1. Joshua 24:15.   7. Matthew 19:17.
2. Matthew 6:24.   8. Romans 7:15,17.
3. John 18:36.   9. Romans 8:7.
4. John 17:15–16.   10. I Corinthians 2:14.
5. Matthew 26:42.   11. I Kings 19:18.
6. John 14:27.

11. Spiritual Supply

1. John 10:30.   3. Luke 15:31.
2. Psalm 24:1.

12. The Power and Dominion

1. John 10:10.   7. John 18:36.
2. John 11:25.   8. Matthew 16:16.
3. Philippians 4:13.   9. John 8:11.
4. John 14:27.   10. John 8:58.
5. John 14:1.   11. Psalm 46:10.
6. Revelation 3:20.

77 10 9 8 7 6 5 4 3